MW00438714

Remarkable Advent

GOD'S EXTRAORDINARY PLAN
THROUGH ORDINARY PEOPLE

Shauna Letellier

© Shauna Letellier

Printed in the United States of America

All rights reserved. No part of this publication may be reproduced, stored in a retrieval system, or transmitted in any form or by any means—electronic, mechanical, photocopy, recording or any other—without prior written permission from the author.

www. shaunaletellier.com

Unless otherwise noted Scripture quotations are taken from the Holy Bible, New International Version®, NIV®. Copyright © 1973, 1978, 1984, 2011 by Biblica, Inc.™ Used by permission of Zondervan. All rights reserved worldwide. www.zondervan.com The "NIV" and "New International Version" are trademarks registered in the United States Patent and Trademark Office by Biblica, Inc.™

Scripture quotations marked (NASB) are taken from the New American Standard Bible®, copyright © 1960, 1962, 1963, 1968, 1971, 1972, 1973, 1975, 1977, 1995 by The Lockman Foundation. Used by permission. www.Lockman.org

Scripture quotations marked (NLT) are taken from The Holy Bible, New Living Translation, copyright © 1996, 2004, 2015 by Tyndale House Foundation. All rights reserved.

Edited by Yolanda Smith.

Cover & interior design by Typewriter Creative Co. Cover illustration by Natalya Antuanetto.

ISBN 978-1-7341374-0-8 (Paperback)
ISBN 978-1-7341374-1-5 (eBook)

She was brave. Only Joseph by her side, a cramped place to give birth, noise everywhere. And more. As she screamed out in pain, the Deceiver stood ready to devour My Son. The heavens shook with war. Michael and his angels reeled. Mighty One do something!

I AM.

—John Blase, *Touching Wonder: Recapturing the Awe of Christmas*

Contents

Introduction

Return to Wonder

We've heard Linus recite it for Charlie Brown. We've acted it out. We've listened to it at church and read it for ourselves. And like Linus, maybe we can even recite it simply because we've listened to it so often.

The Christmas story.

Some have called it, "The Greatest Story Ever Told."

But as with many Bible stories, the colorful images of the Sunday school flannelgraph fade over time. God's eternal and breathtaking story has been reduced to varnished statuettes on the mantel, and the historical windows have frosted, making it difficult to see the context surrounding God's extraordinary work.

Instead of gasping in absolute wonder, we gloss over the words in our Bibles, yawn, lick a finger, and flip the page.

Consumerism encroaches on our evenings and weekends. Our mailboxes and inboxes are filled with Christmas catalogs and seasonal bargains. Children leave long lists in Santa's mailbox at the mall.

The statuettes on the mantel become nothing more than a reminder that we are missing something.

We know it ought to be different. We should be enthralled and not bored with the greatest story ever told.

What if we, as adults, could be fascinated once again with the familiar?

Perhaps we can take some cues from Barbara Robinson's unforgettable characters, the Herdman children. In her story, *The Best Christmas Pageant Ever*, the opening line introduces us to the Herdmans, "the worst kids in the history of the world." All six of them smoked, stole, and fought. And "Since none of the Herdmans had ever gone to church or Sunday school or read the Bible or anything, they didn't know how things were supposed to be."[1]

Then, rehearsal after rehearsal, we watch the uncouth siblings hijack the traditional church Christmas program.

One reason this story clings to the season is because it provides fresh perspective for those of us who are dangerously overfamiliar with the biblical Christmas story. Through the unfiltered outbursts of the irreverent rascals we get to observe the story of Jesus' birth as though we'd never heard it before.

Overfamiliarity causes most of us to yawn through the angel's song and saunter up to the manger unsurprised to find a baby in a feed bucket. Perhaps this year we can take a cue from the Herdmans and un-familiarize ourselves with the Christmas story. Not to forget, but to read it again as if for the first time. A slow and imaginative Bible reading may return the wonder of God's extraordinary plan as we take a fresh look at the familiar.

What if we could stop at history's frosted window and hold a candle there to let the warmth melt the frost and light up the past? We might watch Mary readjust the knot on her belted waist as she trusts God for a future she can't imagine but willingly accepts. We may long to comfort Joseph as he wrestles with what seems to be a terrible nightmare. Perhaps for the first time we will see how God graciously chooses ordinary people to accomplish his extraordinary plan.

In many ways, Zechariah, Elizabeth, Mary, and Joseph were terribly ordinary people hoping for good and noble things—for children, for marriage, for a life pleasing to God, for a king to deliver them from political oppression. But for each of them, God granted life-altering disappointments to shatter their lesser dreams.

None of them could have imagined the critical role they'd play in God's great story. To the old barren couple, he gave a child to prepare the way for The Saving King. To a young teenage couple who were likely labeled adulterers, he granted the grave privilege of raising his Son.

As you look toward Christmas, I invite you to enjoy these daily readings. Each day begins with the framework of scripture, continues with a fictional retelling of one moment in the Christmas story, and concludes with a prayer.

I have tried to stay close to Scripture with these retellings. Where parallel passages were different, I combined the words and accounts of the gospel writers into one. Where Scripture was unclear on motives, I imagined one I felt was reasonable in the situation. Where Scripture was silent, I sifted through possibilities presented in a variety of Bible commentaries. Then I wove in a little historic, geographic, political, religious, and cultural detail to provide context for the passage.

I operated with the understanding that these gospel characters had committed much, if not all, of the first five books of our Bible, as well as the Psalms, to memory. There are occasions inside these chapters where I have inserted dialogue or prayers. Although some do not appear in the biblical accounts, I assumed the person would be familiar with the Scripture and hymn book of their day.

I pray that as we reread the Christmas story as if for the first time, we will be enthralled with our astonishing God, who carries out his extraordinary plan by redeeming the disappointments of ordinary people.

People like you and me.

Righteous and Childless

...his wife Elizabeth was also a descendant of
Aaron. Both of them were righteous in the sight
of God, observing all the Lord's commands and
decrees blamelessly. But they were childless
because Elizabeth was not able to conceive, and
they were both very old."

—Luke 1:5-7

Elizabeth shuffled through the door into her kitchen, a
jar of warm goat's milk on her hip. She filled a cup for
Zechariah and placed it beside his untouched dates and
bread, then slipped out to finish sweeping. The house
was silent except for the swishing broom and the occasional pebble tumbling across the floor.

For more than half a century she had swept floors,
mended garments, woven blankets, fetched the water, ground the grain, and cooked meals for Zechariah.

He loved God, and she loved him for it. But he was no housekeeper. Not at home, anyway. His service was in the temple.

Sweeping dust and crumbs out the front door, she glanced toward Zechariah. He sat hunched at the table, eyes closed, fingers laced, lips moving in silent prayer. The milk cooled beside him as he prepared for his solemn duties at the temple.

His father, as well as hers, had also served there, and from childhood she and Zechariah had been taught the Laws of Moses and the holy requirements of God. Not only was it their heritage, it was also their great privilege.

With reverence they celebrated every feast, hosting family for Passover and facilitating the feast to remember God's deliverance of his people. With gratitude they offered sacrifices as a means of thanks and to be cleansed of sin. With joy they worshiped in song as the great psalms of Asaph reverberated through the temple.

Their hearts were filled with love for God, and their days were filled with service to him.

Twice a year Zechariah served in Jerusalem at the temple for an entire week. This week his division of priests would be on duty.

In just a few moments they would part ways. Zechariah would travel to the temple, and Elizabeth would fetch the water with the other village women.

With the house so quiet, she could hear the women and their gaggle of children walking toward the well. She glanced out the window to gauge her time. While mothers were occupied with empty water jars on heads and hips, the children scampered freely in the road. The happy little brood, always scurrying and scattering, made her giggle. Oh, their energy.

As they neared, two little boys darted from behind their mother and raced toward the edge of the terraced hill. Their mother scolded and called them back, but before obeying, they each hurled a handful of rocks over the edge and listened to them bounce on the boulders below.

Elizabeth gasped at the danger and smiled at their wonder. Bouncing rocks. What a thrill for little ones. She breathed an exhausted sigh at the thought of chasing them away from every danger. Hills, water, fire, animals. Forty years ago, her ache for a child matched her energy and ability to care for one. As the seasons for planting and growth circled in turn, the Earth reproduced its bounty, but Elizabeth remained barren. Years became decades, and God had not blessed them with a child of their own.

It was a bittersweet pleasure to watch a little girl coax a dove toward her hand with a trail of wheat grains, or to see the boys etching game boards in the dirt with sticks and stones. But at her age, she had no business longing for children. She was spent just watching them.

She glanced at Zechariah hoping the children's jolly racket would not disrupt his prayers. But it was too late. His plate was empty. He wiped his mouth and stood to leave.

She kissed him goodbye and watched him amble down the road with the men headed to Jerusalem. She was glad he would have company. And help. Age was slowing them both down.

"God, remember him on his journey," she prayed as she joined the women. She turned again in time to see him hobbling to keep up. *How many more times will he be able to make the journey? And Lord, who will care for me when he's gone?*

She tried to push the nagging thought aside. She knew the Lord would provide for her as he had for their fathers in Egypt and the desert. He had provided a son for Sarah, for Rachel, and for Hannah. But not for her.

A son would have been a fine gift, Lord. She surprised herself with her accusatory tone and then immediately repented. *He is in heaven and I am on earth. I must let my words be few (Ecclesiastes 5:2).*

Hoisting the water jar onto her hip she hummed a psalm she knew well:

Our God is in the heavens, he does whatever he pleases (Psalm 115:3).

She greeted the group of women and their little darlings and fell in step with their lively procession. There was no use guessing how God would provide. She knew his answer would likely be surprising.

∂℞

Poor, dear Zechariah and Elizabeth.

They knew God's law and all the mind-boggling particulars of how to serve God in reverence. In all of this, the gospel writer tells us, they were blameless.

Blameless, but not sinless. Each of them could have enumerated and elaborated on their own sin, and as any married couple, they could have pinpointed other's faults and sins.

But there was no glaring scandal from their household for neighbors to gossip about and no accusations of hypocrisy whispered. If the neighbors were whispering, it was more likely in surprise and pity. Although Zechariah and Elizabeth were blameless in the sight of God, they had no children.

In a time when a woman's value derived from her ability to bear and raise children, and the religious teaching of the day allowed a man to divorce his wife if she could not give him any, the neighbors, not to mention Elizabeth and Zechariah, viewed their childlessness as a great tragedy and probably a means of divine punishment.

Elizabeth must have wondered why God would dangle such a blessing as children—a heritage from the Lord—just out of reach.

She had married the right man, and he the right woman. Their unparalleled devotion to God and anticipation for what he had promised only contributed to the confusion.

The entire Old Testament, with which Zechariah and Elizabeth would have been so familiar, was thick with stories where obedience to God brought blessing and disobedience meant hardship or punishment. Adam and Eve disobeyed God and were forced to leave the garden while Noah, despite the conventional wisdom of the day, obeyed God, built an ark, and was preserved.

Their ancestral history of leadership—kings and judges alike—demonstrated that God prospered the obedient, often by helping them conquer their enemies. But he also punished the disobedient, often by allowing their defeat or capture.

And when their ancestors were enslaved in Egypt, God punished the pharaoh who mistreated them and ushered them to the Promised Land by slicing open the sea and laying road where water had flowed.

Such a clear pattern must have caused the occasional question, "Why, Lord? Why not us? What have we done? What haven't we done?"

"They had waited together these many years," writes Alfred Edersheim, "till in the evening of life the flower of hope had closed its fragrant cup..."[2]

They were regular humans like you and me. Heartache and desire wrestled for prominence in their minds.

For decades they were righteous and childless.

But Zechariah and Elizabeth are proof that it is

possible, by God's grace, to remain faithful to God even when we feel disappointed with his plan.

Righteous and childless.

Disappointed and faithful.

And in for the surprise of their lives.

?

Dear Lord,

You will provide. We have neither the right nor privilege to choose the way, the gift, or the time.

Sometimes the wait is long. While we wait, please give us confidence in your great love and perfect plan. When waiting a day seems like a thousand years, help us remember that someday, a thousand years with you will seem like only a day.

A Bitter Beauty

In the time of Herod king of Judea, there was
a priest named Zechariah who belonged to the
priestly division of Abijah...

—Luke 1:5

Zechariah ambled down the hill country roads of Judea.
A few of the twenty-four priests of his division lived outside of Jerusalem, too. He was grateful for their company today. They made this trip together only twice a year
for their week of service, but with each subsequent journey their steps quickened while his seemed to lag. He
puffed along behind the younger three and occasionally
they would slow.

"Are you doing all right, Zechariah?"

"Oh, yes. No need to wait for me." But they always
did, and he was thankful.

It was normally a two-hour walk, but Zechariah was

feeling his age. He calculated each step, navigating every loose rock and exposed root. Their little band of travelers had stopped to rest in the broad shade of an Acacia tree. Zechariah grabbed a low-hanging branch and steadied himself as he wiped his brow. "Have a drink, Zechariah," the younger priest handed him a skin of water warmed by the sun. Zechariah drank while the others milled about the tree talking, waiting for him, and pointing toward their destination.

Nestled at the base of the hill country lay the jewel of Jerusalem. Even at this distance Zechariah could see gleaming white marble walls of the city, sunlight glinting off golden flourishes at the temple. To Zechariah it was a bitter beauty. The City of God, whose privilege it was to host the Temple of God, was indeed rich and beautiful.

But for Zechariah, its grandeur was dulled by the violent fraud who had constructed Jerusalem's lovely features.

He remembered the political and religious panic among his uncles and father as they watched Herod the Great rise to power some fifty years prior. First in Galilee, and then, after three bloody years, in Jerusalem. An unstoppable devil, Herod did what he pleased, acquired whomever he wanted, and killed whomever he disliked, not sparing his own family.

Zechariah recalled Herod's second marriage to the beautiful Mariamme—Herod's most treasured of several wives. Her advantageous bloodline secured Herod's place with a prominent Jewish family. But as Zechariah and Elizabeth nurtured their own marriage and hoped for children, Herod, in an unjustified rage, executed Mariamme.

Though Rome had appointed him King of the Jews, there was hardly a Jew alive who was not equally terrified and disgusted by Herod. Zechariah and the God-fearing Jews rejected his illegitimate reign, and Herod knew it.

Every political maneuver was meant to magnify himself in hopes of gaining favor with his opponents. He refurbished the sprawling temple complex which emerged as an architectural wonder. His palaces in Jerusalem and Jericho boasted of his self-importance. The monuments and cities built for, and named after, his Roman masters betrayed his true allegiances.

Herod sniffed out every fragrance of vulnerability and used it for his advancement. An earthquake, a drought, a famine. Tragedy was an occasion to exploit desperation and make the people dependent on him.

Every building project, relationship, or military alliance smacked of Herod's attempt to purchase a Jewish loyalty that was not for sale. As with his political hunger, he pursued it with predatory fervor.

For Zechariah, the gleaming marble and golden flourishes of the temple complex, the spires and pools in the walls around the city, and the royal gardens within them were beautiful and bitter.

God had given the land, the marble, the instructions

for construction of the temple and the lush and colorful foliage that adorned it. But it was for Herod's glory that they were designed, and on the backs of an overtaxed populace that they were erected.

The city gates of Jerusalem were, to Zechariah, an entrance to the battleground between two kings. One evil and one infinitely good. One enslaving the people by fear, one promising to free them. One a son of Edom the other a Son of David. One killing his wives and sons, the other promising rescue. One the current ruler, the other yet to come.

Oh, Lord, hurry and send your King. Our Deliverer. Zechariah prayed. His legs burned as he ascended the long ramp leading to the temple complex. If God sent his deliverer today, it would not be a moment too soon. With his creaking joints reminding him of his age, he hoped he would live to see the day.

What a heartache Zechariah must have felt over the decline of his city and nation. With the corrupt politics, the aggrandizing rulers, the maneuvering between them, and the populace either blind to it or terrified by it, Zechariah had reason to despair.

Beyond that, he served in a temple meant for worship

but used for profit. The leadership quarreled over invented doctrines or denied God's revealed truth. They overcharged worshipers for required sacrifices to pad the temple budget. They labored over measuring a tenth of the spices used in the temple but neglected the most important matters—mercy, justice, and faithfulness.

Instead of throwing up his hands, vacating the promised land, or refusing to serve where God had placed him, Zechariah stayed, worshiped God, and fulfilled his God-given assignment. He didn't turn a blind eye to the corruption, but he remained because he loved God and believed he would, one day, send a King to deliver and unify his people. Until then, Zechariah remained faithful even when surrounded by compromising leadership.

Worshiping God in less-than-ideal circumstances is the perfect place to remember that "The Lord does not look at the things people look at. People look at the outward appearance, but the Lord looks at the heart" (1 Samuel 16:7). We can still worship God because, as Jesus pointed out, true worship happens on the inside, regardless of what mountain we're kneeling by or what building we're standing in (See John 4:24).

In the fog of grand-scale apathy, we can still fellowship. We can serve and encourage our brothers and sisters in Christ to believe God will do all he has promised, even when we wonder if he's paying attention. And though we may grow weary, there will be a reward—a harvest the likes of which no eye has seen, no ear has heard, and no mind has conceived. All of it is being prepared by God—over this long and sometimes arduous life—for those who love and trust him (See 1 Corinthians 2:9).

❧

Oh, Lord,

Your every move stands in contrast to our earthly rulers. You did not consider equality with God as something to be held onto, though you certainly had the right to insist.

While kings and kingdoms were serving themselves, you made yourself a servant and became obedient even to the point of dying in the place of those you came to save. Thank you for these glaring distinctions. Make us more like you and less like Herod.

Day 3

Faithful to the Holy

Once when Zechariah's division was on duty and he was serving as priest before God, he was chosen by lot, according to the custom of the priesthood, to go into the temple of the Lord and burn incense.

—Luke 1:8-9

Zechariah rolled over in his bed with a groan and winced. Yesterday's journey to Jerusalem was exhausting. His muscles complained at every movement, but his spirit was eager. *Pity to lie here in the dark when I've traveled all this way to the house of God,* he thought as he propped on his elbow and eased himself upright. Priests who lived in the hill country outside of Jerusalem slept in a series of rooms that formed the interior of the temple walls. Sunlight was scarce there. It made sleep comfortable and waking up difficult.

"This is the day the Lord has made, men," Zechariah announced to his fellow priests to wake them, "Let us rejoice and be glad."[3] He reached for his oil lamp. Its diminishing flame whimpered for more oil, and Zechariah filled it. He proceeded to every man's bedside, topping off each lamp until the room brightened and the men woke.

Despite his aching, the older he got, the more precious the privilege of serving God became.

He thought of Elizabeth, at home alone, and he prayed the Romans would not cause a stir while he was gone. If there was a ruckus, no one was there to comfort or protect her except equally helpless neighbors. Every day, Zechariah and Elizabeth prayed for God to send his Messiah—the king he had promised—to deliver them from the ruling Romans.

But they were still oppressed.

Oppressed, yet provided for. God cared for them, there was no doubt. In their many years of marriage God had seen them through famine and war. They had food and shelter, friends and family.

Still, there was a gaping void. They had prayed for a child of their own, and Zechariah's heart broke with Elizabeth's every month. Together they had repented of sins they could remember and had begged for mercy for sins they might not be aware of. Praying for God to make them holy, they waited and wondered if something they had committed or omitted had closed Elizabeth's womb. What would become of them in their old age?

Who would care for her when he was gone? Who would care for him? And while he knew God would provide, he could not see how.

Zechariah pushed open the heavy wooden door. Massive columns lined the long hallway outside their room, and the purple light of dawn painted them lavender. The same lavender as the flowers, pressed and dried, that would be burned as incense to God this morning—a symbol of their prayers rising to him.

Though the smoke of the incense rose daily with the prayers of citizens and priests, the fragrance hovered below the ceiling. God seemed distant and silent. It had been more than four hundred years since anyone had heard a word from him. But if there was one thing Zechariah had learned from his years in the temple, it was that God delights in doing the unpredictable. One reading through the sacred scrolls was proof. No one could accuse God of operating the usual way.

Distant or not, the beauty of the temple and the meticulous customs were a constant reminder of God's holiness.

After bathing and following every prescribed ritual for ceremonial cleansing, Zechariah joined his division. They went about their task of purifying the holy tools— the censer used for coals and incense, forks and shovels for tending the fires. Twenty-four men divided themselves into two groups equipped with torches to light the lamps.

It was still early, and the courts were dark. But as wicks flickered to life, the seven lamps on each stand found their mirror image in the golden walls. The temple was ablaze with reverence.

Zechariah absorbed the glory of it.

From lamp to lamp, his reflection followed him. A thinning beard hung below his hunched shoulders. Zechariah turned away from the confrontation with the man he knew but barely recognized. An old man with no children and fewer years before him than behind—hardly a worthy servant in this place. The question heaved through his chest unexpectedly, *Why?* Though he'd spent a lifetime confessing sins he wasn't sure he'd committed, he whispered a prayer as familiar as his own name. *Wash me clean from my guilt. Purify me from my sin.*[4]

From every corner of the city, worshipers flocked to the temple, filing in through the gates on all four sides. The Levite choir sang on the steps of the outer court. Zechariah sang along quietly with the chorus and worship flowed freely:

"Lift up your heads, you gates;
lift them up, you ancient doors,
that the King of glory may come in.
Who is he, this King of glory?
The LORD Almighty—
he is the King of glory."[5]

Zechariah and three others finished their tasks and stood shoulder to shoulder in a solemn circle. Before their job was finished, one of them—and only one— would enter the Holy Place to burn the incense and pray. It was a high and holy privilege. The choice was best left to God, so they cast lots.

One man dumped a small pouch of pebbles on the ground. They scattered inside the circle of feet, and a smooth white stone came to rest in front of Zechariah.

He gasped.

He'd served most of his life and had never been chosen for this supreme moment. The opportunity would never come again, and he understood the gravity.

Immediately he began to mentally rehearse the particulars of his responsibility. He would bring the special incense, a recipe prescribed by God himself, to burn on the golden altar. While doing so, he would pray on behalf of Israel and then, when he was done, he would speak a blessing over the worshipers outside.

It was not a strenuous privilege, but to perform it in the wrong way, or with unconfessed sin in his heart, was an offense to the God he sought to worship. He recalled Israel's history when the sons of Aaron disobeyed God as they performed the same duty. Irreverence and a flippancy toward God's holiness had cost them their lives. God consumed them with fire in an instant, and their charred bodies were dragged from the Holy Place and left outside the camp.

A holy God required holy servants.

Zechariah trembled and prayed, "Search me, God, and know my heart; test me and know my anxious thoughts. See if there is any offensive way in me, and lead me in the way everlasting."[6]

The fire was kindled in the altar, and Zechariah was left alone in the Holy Place hugging the jar of incense. The thick curtain behind him muffled the courtyard music. With the golden table to his right and the lamp stand illuminating the room on his left, he moved solemnly toward the altar. He mixed the dried flowers and herbs with the coals, and fragrance filled the room. Zechariah bowed his heart and asked God to prepare the way for the consolation of Israel.

❦

What reverence and fear the priests of Zechariah's division must have felt.

And if not, they certainly should have.

As descendants of Aaron, their duty was to attend the meticulous, logistical matters of worshiping a perfectly holy God.

But God, in his all-knowing mercy, sees beyond ritualistic particulars straight into the heart. The two sons of Aaron who were in some way inattentive and irreverent offered "strange fire" (Leviticus 10:1). The unauthorized "strange fire" was merely the evidence that their hearts were estranged from God.

Zechariah's heart was not.

With such humility, Zechariah might have hoped to perform his duty and retreat from the frightening holiness of God, knowing that at any moment he could mess things up.

With a cautious eye towards his tendency for routine worship, Zechariah likely saw his own unworthiness—in a once-in-a-lifetime way—reflected off the golden walls of the Holy place. It was a place he would never see again, but one he would never forget.

While we might feel a little sorry for Zechariah's reverent fear, this is exactly where God meant for him to be. A heart that acknowledges its tendency for casual worship can also ask God for help and grace to ascribe the reverence he is due. And the one who clings to God in reverence will find herself pulled close to the Father.

And that's a pretty good place to be.

Dear Lord,

How can we comprehend the scope of your holiness? In long silences and oppressive circumstances, you remain perfectly holy. Give us hearts to serve you willingly, humbly, and with the reverence you are due.

Day 4

A Silenced Skeptic

"Then an angel of the Lord appeared to him, standing at the right side of the altar of incense. When Zechariah saw him, he was startled and was gripped with fear... Meanwhile, the people were waiting for Zechariah and wondering why he stayed so long in the temple. When he came out, he could not speak to them. They realized he had seen a vision in the temple, for he kept making signs to them but remained unable to speak."

—Luke 1:11-22

A sudden breeze pushed his beard to one side.

The sound of enormous wings settling into place startled him.

Zechariah jumped and opened his eyes to too much

bright light.

He mumbled a plea for mercy as he staggered backward.

Before him stood a creature like nothing he'd ever seen. Gold and lightning, bronze and fire had all collided into a man. When Zechariah's eyes had adjusted to the tremendous brightness, he could see a resemblance to carvings in the wood and gold of the temple.

But this was no carving. Afraid to look upward, Zechariah kept his eyes on a hem of crisp, white linen and the tail end of a golden sash swaying in the unexplainable breeze.

Trembling, he reached to steady himself, but found nothing.

Surely, he had offended God. Offered the wrong coals, or the wrong incense, or entered with the wrong heart. Death by radiance would be his end.

Zechariah raised his forearm to shield his eyes. His sleeve was no protection from the brilliance. His knees buckled and slammed onto the marble floor.

A voice spoke. "Do not be afraid, Zechariah; your prayer has been heard."

He peeked from behind his translucent sleeve. *My prayer? Which one?* he wanted to ask, but holy fear left him speechless.

As if answering the unspoken inquiry, the angel spoke again, "Your wife Elizabeth will have a son and you will name him John."

Zechariah gathered himself from the floor, straightened his aching knees, and tried to stand. He could not believe his ears. This angel called him by name. Knew his wife. Knew of their childless home.

The angel continued, "Your son John will be a joy and a delight to you and Elizabeth. In fact, many will rejoice because of his birth. He will be great in the sight of the Lord."

Zechariah stood in stunned silence. *At his age? A son? John?*

"But you must teach him that he is never to take wine or any other fermented drink. And he will be filled with the Holy Spirit even from his birth."

Zechariah couldn't take it in. *Filled with the Holy Spirit from birth?* Who had heard of such things?

From the overflow of his doubting heart Zechariah whispered bold words. "How can I be sure of this?" He looked down at his swollen knuckles and crooked fingers holding the empty incense jar. "I am an old man," he paused, "and my wife ... she is well along in years."

But surely the angel knew. It was too late. The words were out.

Undaunted, the angel replied, "I am Gabriel."

Zechariah swallowed hard. The incense caught between his nostrils and his chest. *Gabriel? The one who spoke centuries ago to the prophet Daniel?*

"I stand in the presence of God, and he has sent me to tell you this good news. I can do nothing but say what is true. Because you don't believe me, you will be silent and unable to speak until the day this all happens. And believe me, these things *will* come true at their proper time."

Zechariah squinted through the smoke of the incense as the dim flicker of the lamp became the primary light in the holy room.

The angel was gone.

Zechariah turned and scanned the small space. Yes. He was alone.

What now?

With unsteady steps he hobbled toward the curtain to finish his duty. The people were awaiting the blessing. Shooting pain in his knees made him dizzy. Perhaps it was the potent incense, or the smoke that had set his head spinning. Maybe his old eyes were still adjusting.

Zechariah emerged from the Holy Place and faced the restless crowd. Upon seeing him, they settled. The choir turned on the steps to face him, and his fellow priests nodded urgently, *Go on.*

Zechariah opened his mouth to speak the blessing, but nothing came.

Another priest came closer to hear. He pleaded with Zechariah to finish, but he could not utter a word.

Gabriel had gone, but his promise had stayed.

Zechariah pointed to the curtain behind him to explain to the other priests. Their furrowed brows told him that his delay was unappreciated. He tried again, discretely flapping his arms, and was embarrassed at his ridiculous display. Pointing again, he mimicked his spreading the incense and feigned a startled expression.

A vague understanding settled among them. His trembling evidenced something exceptional. Another priest volunteered to pronounce the blessing on the curious worshipers.

Zechariah stepped away from the others. He pushed a sweaty fist into his chest to calm the wild pounding. With the other hand he covered his quivering mouth.

The angel's words echoed off the walls of his mind.

Silent and unable to speak.

Finally, he understood. This was confirmation of a bigger surprise. For Israel and for Elizabeth.

Oh Elizabeth! He could not wait to tell...

Well, God would help him find a way.

Isn't it just like God to wait to do what only he can be credited for?

He will not yield his glory to another (See Isaiah 42:8). Just when Zechariah and Elizabeth have come to grips with the fact that their bodies are as good as dead for reproduction, just when they've learned to live with heartsickness over deferred hope, God sets his wild plan in motion.

And, as he would have it, his plan is about to fulfill a heart-wrenching desire and a desperate need. Not only for Zechariah and Elizabeth, but also for a nation and a world aching for rescue.

It's certainly not impossible for God to send an angel to notify you that your prayer has been answered. The writer of Hebrews tells us that some of us have shown hospitality to angels without even realizing it (See Hebrews 13:2). But we must be cautious not to demand extraordinary signs from God in exchange for our trust in him. He is trustworthy regardless. God remains true to his word whether we see it or not, whether we believe it or not. "If we are faithless, He remains faithful, for He cannot deny Himself " (2 Timothy 2:13, NASB).

We trust him to remedy the most desperate need of humanity because he said he would. He will save his people from their sins. God's people waited millennia to see their Rescuer. They forgot God in the meantime and became, quite literally, heartsick.

"Hope deferred makes the heart sick, but a longing fulfilled becomes a tree of life" (Proverbs 13:12). It grows and flourishes to prepare for another Branch rooted in a stump God's people thought was as good as dead—the root of Jesse (See Isaiah 11:1).

On this side of history, we have the great privilege of knowing that Israel's longing, and God's promise, has been completed in Jesus. He is God's provision for the clean heart David requested in his ancient song. Jesus is God's answer to Zechariah's intercession in the Holy Place. Jesus' work on our behalf is the fulfillment of God's promise to save.

God saw fit to inform an old, heart-sick priest that a tree of life was about to bud. And Zechariah's son would cultivate the ground and prepare the way for him.

❧

Dear Lord,

Give us holy reverence for your wild and sovereign ways.

Grant us childlike faith to believe what you have spoken in your Word, and to give you glory for what only you can do.

Day 5

Home

When his time of service was completed, he returned home. After this his wife Elizabeth became pregnant and for five months remained in seclusion. "The Lord has done this for me," she said. "In these days he has shown his favor and taken away my disgrace among the people."

—Luke 1:23-24

Zechariah woke to the first rays of sunlight peeking between the curtains and streaming directly into his eyes. Elizabeth lay beside him, her breathing long and slow. He rubbed the brightness from his eyes and climbed from bed to close the curtain. Below the window he noticed the neighbor's chickens. They scratched for grain and flew at one another in a fury of greed. Sticking his arm through the curtain, he waved and scattered them.

Take your noise home, he thought. Elizabeth had been so tired in the weeks since he'd returned from Jerusalem, he was glad she was still sleeping.

Zechariah ambled to the stove and lit a fire. He placed the last of yesterday's water to boil then sat in his chair to pray and promptly fell asleep. He woke with a start to a hand on his shoulder. Their young neighbor woman smiled down at him as he slumped. He straightened and watched her lips. She was shaking her head and probably apologizing for waking him, but he heard nothing. Holding up her water jar, she raised her eyebrows and slowly mouthed the syllables, *Is Elizabeth going for water today?*

Zechariah shook his head. No. Elizabeth would not be fetching water this morning. She hadn't in five months. Sometimes the village women brought water, sometimes Zechariah went to the well himself. As the neighbor left, she removed his water pot from the cooling stove and set it on the table. Zechariah followed her to the door as if he'd been the most attentive host and closed it behind her. On the table sat the water pot, hot and empty. He'd have to fetch more when it cooled.

Grabbing the broom, he began to sweep pebbles toward the door. He'd done the best he could to explain to their family, neighbors, and to Elizabeth. He longed to tell her the angel's exact words—that their little boy would be devoted to God's Messiah. Zechariah had even written *John* with the ashen end of a stick from the fire.

She had picked up bits of Hebrew lettering over the years, but she could not read it. Instead, Zechariah had reenacted his encounter with the angel, imitating his own terrifying surprise, pointing to her tummy, waddling around their house, and rocking a loaf of bread in his arms. After the nausea began, she stayed home and worshipped. She finally understood.

At least in part.

He finished sweeping. Elizabeth was awake now. Bowed in her chair, eyes closed, lips moving. He laid a hand on hers, and she opened her eyes. Seeing the water jar under his arm she nodded, and he left.

Though his feet and ankles always ached, his sore muscles had adapted, and the hike to and from the well got a little easier each time.

The promised silence had been an unlikely blessing for them both. There was much he could not do. Invitations to discuss civil and theological matters stopped coming. No one asked for advice or prayer. And while it was a source of sorrow, it freed him to serve his weary wife. Busy days were ahead, and rest would be scarce.

God was going to give them a son. His name meant, "God is Gracious." When they said goodnight or woke him, when they called him for meals—every time they spoke his name—they would declare what God had done. God was indeed gracious. Not only to them, but to the entire nation. Gabriel said John would turn many of their people back to God, to prepare them for their long-awaited Messiah. Four hundred years ago the prophet Malachi had spoken of it:

"I will send my messenger, who will prepare the way..." (Malachi 3:1).

Zechariah shook his head as he walked. The prophet had spoken of their son. *Their son.* Emotion choked him every time he thought of it, and Elizabeth had noticed. She'd rub his shoulders thinking him to be in pain and press her cheek to his. He'd smile and shake his head. Someday soon he would tell her the whole story through a shower of relieved tears.

ॐ

Divine discipline is difficult. The writer of Hebrews tells us, "No discipline is pleasant at the time..." (Hebrews 12:11). But oh, how it is our friend, our guide, and a great mercy in keeping us from future wrong. It eventually produces the peaceful fruit of righteousness.

If Zechariah had emerged from the Holy Place with full voice and spoken all that was expected of him, he surely would have given the other priests and the people a wild-eyed account of what happened behind the curtain.

Considering the infrequency of God's noticeable intervention during that time in biblical history, and the fact that he hadn't spoken through prophets for a long time, Zechariah's truthful account would have been an unbelievable explanation for his tardiness in pronouncing the blessing.

His fellow priests might have whispered, "Ridiculous," and then felt his forehead, insisting he retire from his priestly duties early that night—possibly forever.

But God's discipline is also merciful. It kept Zechariah from additional verbal missteps and cured his unbelief.

God relieved him of the responsibility of convincing his fellow priests of what he had seen. "Because of his silence, they realized he had seen a vision in the temple" (Luke 1:22).

It was also merciful, preliminary proof to Elizabeth that something big was in the works. Just as Zechariah might doubt his memory and wonder, "Am I making this up?" he would attempt to voice his concerns to Elizabeth and be reminded that, no he was not.

We are not so different from Zechariah. The writer of Hebrews tells us that when we endure discipline, "God is treating you as sons. For what son is there whom his father does not discipline?" (Hebrews 12:11).

In our own unbelief we often echo the same question, "God, how can that possibly be true? Help me in my unbelief." But let us not take offence when he answers by applying his merciful discipline.

Though the discipline is unpleasant at the time, it is proof that we belong to him. He is our living, intervening Father, and we can believe his every word.

❧

Dear Lord,

Thank you for your gracious discipline. Though we have no right to doubt your word, we sometimes do. But you love us too much to let us wallow in unbelief.

Give us eyes to see your hidden grace and hearts prepared to praise you when we finally see that even in your judgment, there is mercy.

An Inconceivable Conception

In the sixth month of Elizabeth's pregnancy, God sent the angel Gabriel to Nazareth, a town in Galilee, to a virgin pledged to be married to a man named Joseph, a descendant of David. The virgin's name was Mary... "I am the Lord's servant," Mary answered. "May your word to me be fulfilled."

—Luke 1:26-38

A spring wind rolled across the plain and gusted upward as it collided with Mount Tabor. Nestled at its base was a little village, not unknown, but also not properly enjoyed. Nazareth was nothing more than an obstacle to travelers on the well-worn passage between the Sea of

Galilee and the Great Mediterranean Sea. But to Mary it was home.

The fragrance of almond blossoms breezed through her window whipping up a fine dust of freshly ground flour.

Mary breathed a bit too quickly and inhaled a wisp of it. She coughed, caught her breath, and returned to the tempo of her work. She moved her hand rhythmically as she ground the wheat. The scraping stone was a suitable instrument, and after her throat cleared, she began to hum.

With her mother gone to the spring and her father working in the groves of almonds, it was especially easy to lose herself in song. No one interrupted her melody. No one slowed her work. No one critiqued her worship.

It was a favorite song she'd learned on their last trip to Jerusalem for Passover.

Of course, the scraping rhythm of stone on wheat was not the cheery jingle of the tambourine-playing travelers, but it was efficient, helping her work and worship at the same time.

"If your sons keep my covenant
and the statutes I teach them,
then their sons will sit
on your throne for ever and ever."[7]

She smiled at the lyrics and envisioned her future with Joseph. He was a righteous man who would someday teach their children to love and obey God. Someday, their children would climb in his lap and hear the stories of how God had delivered their ancestors from enemies by the sling of young David. Joseph would recount the story of God's hand parting the Red Sea and laying a path right through it. And Mary would listen too and marvel that God always keeps his promises.

But in the distance between then and now, she felt pressure to master her homemaking skills throughout this year preceding their marriage. She paid careful attention to the consistency of the flour she dumped in her wooden bowl. Her last batch of bread had been coarse and dry. And while her family had politely choked it down, she was determined to make a loaf they would enjoy.

Mary prayed silently. "God, make me a suitable helper for Joseph."

The wind gusted, toppling an empty jar on the sill. It crashed to the floor. Mary gasped and inhaled flour and dust. Light filled the room. Had the lamp spilled oil and fire? Had the broken jar burst into flames? Mary shielded her eyes. The shards were not burning, but the room was ablaze.

"Greetings, favored one. The Lord is with you."

Mary dropped the grindstone.

At first, she could not see him. She squinted into the brightness. His face was like lightning and his eyes like flames.

He bent down, picked up the grindstone, and handed it back to her.

Too breathless to speak, and too weak to move, Mary only stared. He laid the grindstone in the bowl.

Kneeling to her level, his voice softened, "Don't be afraid, Mary. You have found favor with God."

What? Why? She looked around frantically to see if anyone else had come in to explain.

No one but an angel.

"Mary, God has chosen you to be the mother of his son. And he wants you to name him Jesus."

Jesus? She blinked and shook her head to wake herself. But she was not asleep.

He continued, "Jesus will be great. In fact, he'll be called 'Son of the Most High.' The Lord your God laid plans to give him the throne of his father David and make him ruler forever. But he will have a new kind of kingdom. An everlasting one."

Mary nodded slightly. She recognized the description from hundreds of scriptures read to her and the songs she had sung her whole life. *The Son of David. The Messiah.*

She looked down at her intertwined and trembling fingers. She had just one question, if she could find the breath to ask. "How will this happen?" she whispered. "I'm not married yet, and I've never been with a man."

She stared into the ordinary hands of the Messiah's mother.

"This will not come about in the usual way, Mary. The Holy Spirit will come upon you and the Most High God will overshadow you. He will put the baby in your womb so the child born to you will be holy. In this way, he will be called the Son of God.

"As a matter of fact," he added, "your cousin Elizabeth is going to have a baby, too. Even in her old age, the one they called 'childless' is already in her sixth month."

Under raised brow, Mary's curiosity turned her face upward. *A baby for Elizabeth too? But she is...*

The angel smiled, "Remember, Mary, nothing is impossible for God."

Wide-eyed and willing, Mary replied, "I am the Lord's servant. May it be to me as you have said."

⁂

Mary probably expected a young Jewish woman to be the mother of the Messiah, but it's quite unlikely she ever dreamed it would be her.

Kings were born to royal families in royal towns. Not to nobodies at roadside rest stops.

But isn't it just like God to reveal his plan to those we might consider "weak" and "foolish"? As a teenager, Mary hadn't been lured into laughable skepticism by a lifetime of harsh realities. She did not have sixty years of "unanswered" prayers filed away in heaven to be answered later as Zechariah and Elizabeth did.

And though she didn't fully understand, she didn't

doubt. Her question is wonder. "How can this be because I am a virgin?" There is the hint of eager desire to participate in God's plan.

Mary demonstrates the contrast of humble belief *(That sounds amazing, how will it happen?)* to Zechariah's skeptical doubt *(That sounds ridiculous, how can it be?).* It differentiates the Lord's weary servant from his willing one.

For he has chosen the foolish, weak, unlikely and willing ones of this world so that when he fulfills his plan in and through you and me, we can only boast that God's strength was made perfect in our weakness (See 2 Corinthians 12:9).

And it is only by his strengthening power that we can say with Mary, "I am the Lord's servant. May it be to me as you have said."

Dear Lord,

Give us a heart like Mary's. An expectant heart that believes your promises and awaits their fulfillment. A humble heart that realizes nothing can be done to earn your favor.

Help us follow her example and place

ourselves in your hands. Whether it means public scrutiny, or the death of our own contrived ways, help us consider the supremacy of your inconceivable plan.

Day 7

An Unbelievable Predicament

...Then the angel left her.

—Luke 1:38

Mary picked up the grindstone because she didn't know what else to do. Her hands shook. The grindstone felt like an anchor instead of an instrument. She stared at the place where the angel had been. Shards of the broken jar lay scattered across the floor. *What had just happened?*

As she stood to grab the broom, she stepped on the edge of the bowl full of flour. It catapulted a powdery blast onto her feet and across the room. A morning's work floating through the sunlight and settling on every surface. She swept the dirty flour and the shattered pottery into a powdery heap.

The angel's words collided in her mind like the echoes of elated children hollering in a canyon. *Favored one... you will bear a son... name him Jesus... Son of God... eternal kingdom. Nothing will be impossible with God. Even for Elizabeth in her old age...*[8]

For most of her life Mary's family had remembered her cousin Elizabeth in their prayers, asking God to bless her with children. When had they all stopped praying? Mary couldn't remember. And now, so many years later, the answer had come. If she was six months along as the angel had said, she would need help preparing for the baby. Even young mothers needed help. And Elizabeth ... well, there would be much to do.

It was at least a week's journey south to Zechariah and Elizabeth's home in the hill country outside of Jerusalem. If Mary traveled with a large group, it could take longer. But if she left in the morning, she might arrive in time to help Elizabeth prepare for the Sabbath.

Questions piled up like the broken jar she was pushing around the floor with her broom. What about Joseph? He was working so hard to prepare a place they could share after their marriage.

How could she explain? Mary knew the prophet Daniel had been visited by angels. Jacob had seen hosts of them on a ladder leaning on the edge of heaven. But she was not a prophet or patriarch. No one in her family had ever spoken of a personal angelic visitation. Who would believe that an angel had stood right in front of the stove, outshining the fire, and making such an announcement?

And what on earth would she say to Elizabeth when she arrived? *Hello Elizabeth, I had a visit from an angel last week.*

And Zechariah? He was a priest. If she told him of an angel, what on earth would he say? But she was compelled to go and see them. A baby was on the way! Could her parents object to her desire to help?

Her hands were sticky with sweat and caked flour. Mary washed up and went to find a small blanket. Spreading it on her bed, she began to pack a few things before her parents arrived home.

They would never believe it. At least not until her body began showing signs. But then, their only reasonable assumption would be adultery—not divine favor. Mary pressed her fingers to her temples. She shut her eyes, inhaled and waited for God to calm her.

You will keep him in perfect peace

whose mind is stayed on you,

because he trusts in you. (Isaiah 26:3)

She replayed every unimaginable detail.

The angel's declaration echoed. *Nothing is impossible for God.*

She believed him and finished her packing.

If only the angel would have stayed a while longer. At least until her parents got home or until Joseph stopped by. Gabriel could have left her with some merciful, immediate sign as he had for Zechariah. A sign would have caused her parents or Joseph to inquire about what remarkable thing had happened. Perhaps a swatch of his golden sash? Or a signed celestial affidavit to corroborating Mary's account of their conversation?

But all Mary had to show for her encounter was pale-faced wonder and an urgent desire to see Elizabeth.

While Zechariah walked out of the Holy Place mute but convinced, Mary retained the privilege of speech and persuaded her parents she needed to visit Elizabeth. Once she arrived in the hill country of Judea, her cousin's protruding belly would be confirmation of God's blessing.

The angel left, and she still had her full voice. The only thing that had changed was Mary's entire perception of her future. She had likely dreamed of being a wife and mother. But mother of the Messiah? She wouldn't have dreamt it possible. No, the angel didn't leave an immediate sign, but he left her with the promise that all things are possible with God.

The angel was specific about some details. You will conceive a Son. You will name him Jesus. He will reign forever. The Holy Spirit will come upon you. He will be called the Son of God. Elizabeth is pregnant.

But he was also vague. He didn't tell her exactly what to do next. The flour still had to be ground. She still had to clean up her mess. With trembling hands and churning stomach, she did her ordinary chores as she pondered the great privilege God had given and what she ought to do.

Don't you and I wobble under the same tension? God has given many specific directives. Turn from sin. Love God. Love one another. Pray for your enemies. Care for the needy. And yet sometimes the how-to specifics seem vague.

Often, the next thing we need to do is remember what God has already said. To Mary it came as an angelic messenger declaring the impossible: a virgin and an old woman will bear children.

To us, God's declarations come through the Bible. As we read, we find he is faithful to do all he's promised. To our great relief, God has given us the Holy Spirit to guide and direct in our individual lives. His Spirit is our Teacher and Reminder (John 14:26). He is our Helper, Counselor, and Comforter (John 14:16).

When we don't know what to do next, we can echo the words of the frightened Israelites, "We do not know what to do, but our eyes are on you." (2 Chronicles 20:12). And by keeping him in our sights, we necessarily follow his leading whether he ushers us into the hill country or asks us to stay right where we are.

❦

Dear Lord,

Thank you for strategically orchestrating every detail, even the ones that appear to be obstacles. Thank you for the gifts you give to confirm your work in our lives. In our confused stewing, help us trust your unseen plan, and show us what to do next. May every step be evidence of faith-filled obedience to you.

Day 8

Hill Country Reprieve

At that time Mary got ready and hurried to a town in the hill country of Judea, where she entered Zechariah's home and greeted Elizabeth. When Elizabeth heard Mary's greeting, the baby leaped in her womb, and Elizabeth was filled with the Holy Spirit. "...As soon as the sound of your greeting reached my ears, the baby in my womb leaped for joy. Blessed is she who has believed that the Lord would fulfill his promises to her!"

—Luke 1:39-45

Mary was spent. The pace was faster than she had expected given the number of people traveling in the caravan. She plodded along steadily but with heavy feet. She hadn't filled her water pouch since yesterday morning, but she was almost there.

She knew the route well. Every year during Passover her family stayed with Zechariah and Elizabeth. The familiar sights in the hill country outside of Jerusalem quickened her step and just before sundown, she stood in front of their house.

Mary rapped on the door and peeked through the window. Zechariah was slumped in a chair. His arms were crossed over his belly and his beard draped over his arms. Beard, arms and belly rose and fell with each slow breath. Elizabeth was bent over a table rolling out dough, her belly obscured by the folds of her robe.

Mary knocked again and pushed the door open slowly. "Hello... Elizabeth?"

Elizabeth dropped the roller, grabbed her swollen belly, and let out a joyful cry. She rushed toward Mary. Her lip quivered, and her aged eyes were glassy with fresh tears. She laughed as she kissed Mary's forehead then wrapped her in a hug.

Mary felt Elizabeth's protruding tummy pressing into her own. Her sixth month, indeed.

Elizabeth grasped Mary's shoulders. Tears spilled over now, but her face was peaceful and resolved. She knew Elizabeth would welcome her visit, but she had not expected such an emotional reunion. She cried and laughed loudly. *A woman without pretense,* Mary marveled.

"Mary, you have been blessed by God. And the child in your womb is the blessed Messiah! But why am I so favored that the mother of my Lord should visit me?"

Before she could say, "an angel visited me," Elizabeth cupped Mary's face with floured hands and kissed both cheeks in turn.

"But how did you..." Mary stammered.

"I know you're carrying the Messiah, Mary, because as soon as I heard your greeting, the baby in my womb leaped for joy."

She hugged Mary again, almost as if to introduce the baby cousins.

Mary couldn't find words. She had believed the angel, but she had thought she'd have to convince Elizabeth. But it was Elizabeth who was declaring to her that she was indeed carrying God's Messiah. God was set on proving himself true. His presence was palpable. None of it was a made-up dream, and Elizabeth knew it. Even Elizabeth's baby acknowledged the miracle. Heavy reverence settled on Mary, and she hardly knew what to say.

"What about you?" Mary asked. "You're six months along already?"

"Oh, Mary," Elizabeth's voice softened, "The Lord has done this for me. He has shown me his favor and has taken away my disgrace among the people. For five months I didn't leave the house because I couldn't stop worshiping him."

Mary scanned the room for a place to sit. She was weak with holy awe.

Elizabeth supported her arm with one hand and tipped

her chin with the other. "Blessed is she who believed what the Lord has said to her will be accomplished." Elizabeth led her to a chair by the fire. Zechariah didn't stir.

God was doing all he had promised so many centuries ago. Scriptures declaring his promises and mercy flooded Mary's mind and then pooled in her heart. Out of the overflow, she worshiped:

> "My soul glorifies the Lord
> and my spirit rejoices in God my Savior,
> for he has been mindful
> of the humble state of his servant.
> From now on all generations will call me blessed,
> for the Mighty One has done great things for me—
> holy is his name.
> His mercy extends to those who fear him,
> from generation to generation.
> He has performed mighty deeds with his arm;
> he has scattered those who are proud in their inmost thoughts.
> He has brought down rulers from their thrones
> but has lifted up the humble.
> He has filled the hungry with good things
> but has sent the rich away empty.
> He has helped his servant Israel,
> remembering to be merciful
> to Abraham and his descendants forever,
> just as he promised our ancestors."
> (Luke 1:46-56)

Elizabeth wiped her eyes. "Yes, Mary. This is our God." She patted Zechariah's knee until one eye cracked open. Seeing Mary sitting across from him, he startled, maneuvered himself to a more dignified position in his chair, and blinked. Elizabeth looked him straight in the face and enunciated, "It's Mary. My cousin Mary."

He nodded and smiled and held out his arms for her to come close. His hands trembled a bit, but Mary couldn't be sure if it was his age or the fact the Elizabeth had just thrust him from sleep to hosting company. Taking Mary's face in his hands, he greeted her, not with words of grace and peace, but with a kiss on each cheek.

"He hasn't spoken in six months." Elizabeth sighed. "But he knows God's work is at hand."

❧

Mary's head must have been positively swimming, and yet, she was clear on one thing: She believed God.

She was an obscure young lady from an insignificant village where nothing extraordinary happened. As far as Nazareth knew, nothing out of the ordinary had happened still. But for Mary, God's extraordinary plan had catapulted her into firm belief.

God was teaching a most unlikely player in his great story about himself. With every conversation in that quiet house in the Judean hill-country, God confirmed to Mary what his word had already taught her.

I am sovereign. I have a plan. I choose the unlikely. I do the unthinkable, and I am faithful to fulfill every extraordinary and inconceivable promise I make. And I will do every last bit of it in my way and in my timing.

I will confirm that I have put a child in your womb before you even have a recognizable symptom. I will assure you, through a woman who loves me and knows you, that indeed you are carrying the child that generations have been waiting for. He is the King I have promised. I will be his Father. You will be his mother.

You are willing, and I am able.

With such ongoing intervention and communication from an unseen God, it's no wonder a lifetime of memorized scriptures and synagogue readings would have converged in Mary's head and poured from her mouth.

This is the same God we serve. He can mute a priest and prompt a young girl to compose a song no one had yet heard.

He is our God.

He is able. We must be willing.

And as we watch him work, our natural response is worship.

Oh, Lord,

Thank you that your Word is as good as done. Your methods are astonishing and brilliant and accomplish so much more than our small minds can conceive.

May we, like Mary, be willing vessels of your work and an instrument to sing your praise.

Day 9

An Old New Mama

When it was time for Elizabeth to have her baby, she gave birth to a son. Her neighbors and relatives heard that the Lord had shown her great mercy, and they shared her joy.

—Luke 1:57

Elizabeth had been pacing, then doubling over, all morning. Mary walked with her, stopped to support her, gave her a drink, and guided her to a chair. Then, restless with pain, Elizabeth got up and asked for another walk.

Mary's hands were slick with sweat. So were Elizabeth's. Zechariah had rushed to get the midwife and had been gone so long Mary worried he hadn't been able to communicate the urgency. *God, bring them soon,* Mary pleaded.

Elizabeth held her breath and then, with an excruciating exhale, sat down.

Mary heard the door, and the midwife hurried in. *Oh, thank you, God.*

The midwife was all scowls and concentration. She brushed Mary aside, and demanded Elizabeth get up from the chair and slow her breathing. Instead, Elizabeth's shoulders lurched as she let out one great sob. Mary was startled. The midwife showed so little concern for Elizabeth's suffering. How much more could a woman her age survive? *Is this how life comes, God? With sweat and blood and crying?*

The midwife readied the birthing stool, and Mary stood in a corner. Shaking. Nauseated. Witnessing a birth.

Elizabeth cried out as the midwife barked instructions. Mary found herself crying too. It looked hard. And painful. And scary. *I am the Lord's servant.* She recalled her bold and believing words. She'd seen and heard women in labor before but knowing it would soon be her turn gave her fresh fright.

After what seemed an eternity, the midwife, in one swooping motion, pulled the wailing baby into the world. She wiped his nose and mouth, toweled him mostly clean, and plopped him, squirming and naked, into Elizabeth's arms.

In her exhaustion, Elizabeth could only weep.

As the baby declared his arrival with tiny wailing, Mary heard Zechariah shuffling wall to wall in the other room.

Mary summoned all her trembling courage and

stepped from the corner. She helped the midwife with the sopping and soiled rags.

In her single act of tenderness, the midwife covered Elizabeth and the baby with blankets, and Mary wondered if Elizabeth was already asleep. Elizabeth lifted a weary hand and motioned for Mary to come close.

The baby was wrapped in a cocoon of linen and tucked in Elizabeth's arms. With his eyes squeezed shut and his mouth pursed, he looked incapable of the squalling she'd heard a moment ago. She ran the back of her finger against his chubby cheek. The corner of his mouth twitched, and she thought he might have smiled.

Tears welled in her eyes, and love welled in her heart.

She loved Elizabeth—a gracious, godly woman, who was not merely a relative but, despite her age, had become almost a sister to her. Mary wished Elizabeth could come back to Nazareth with her. For only Elizabeth understood a miraculous pregnancy and believed in angelic messengers.

And, Mary already loved the sweet baby—a cousin to hers. She ran fingertips over his silky black hair.

What a pair they will make.

On John the Baptist's birthday, it was as if God thumbed through the celestial file drawer labeled "Prayers to be

Answered When the Time Has Come" and withdrew the folder of one blameless couple to begin checking off their requests with affirmative answers. Prayers for children combined with prayers for a nation, fitted together with prayers for deliverance, all made in accordance with God's will and promise. On this day, God's "Not yet" became "Today's the day."

God plans his purposes. At the perfect time he provides what he determines we need, sometimes even before we think to ask for it. "For your Father knows what you need before you ask him" (Matthew 6:8).

But when we articulate our needs and desires in conversation with our able God, his answers, even when decades intervene, are gifts to remind us that he hears.

Because of a request for confirmation, God directed Mary to Elizabeth. There she received a three-month intensive education on homemaking, pregnancy, labor, delivery, and the proper care of a newborn boy. And though she didn't yet know it, she would need to explain it all to Joseph between contractions and labored breathing.

Through five months of solitary worship God gave Elizabeth words to confirm for Mary that she was indeed pregnant. Mary's story about Gabriel's startling appearance and declaration surely filled in some blanks for Elizabeth who still hadn't received the full account from Zechariah. And before Elizabeth knew the absolute exhaustion of the third trimester at an age that was considered "beyond child-bearing years," God sent an energetic young woman eager to test her home making skills and gobble up every bit of wisdom.

God is the same today, tomorrow, and forever, and because he is, he will do the same for you and me. When questions and confusion drive us to "pray in the Spirit on all occasions with all kinds of prayers and requests" (Ephesians 6:18), we may not hear the answer we had hoped for, but we will find him—listening, caring, and providing in unexpected ways.

God has holy reasons to wait while we are begging, as he did for Elizabeth, and to go ahead before we are ready, as he did for Mary.

As we obey and worship him, he directs, educates, and provides for his plan which is never limited by what we cannot conceive.

⁂

Dear Lord,

To an old woman you sent a young helper. And to a teenage girl, in a season of lonely obedience, you gave a wise and willing guide.

Before we know what to ask, you already have an efficient and unimaginable plan in motion. You are a gracious provider.

A Name Game

On the eighth day they came to circumcise the child, and they were going to name him after his father Zechariah...

—Luke 1:59

Elizabeth propped her newborn on her shoulder. She cradled his bottom and patted his back to the beat of his breathing. His tummy was full now. Rhythmic breaths pulsed against her neck as he drifted into sleep. She closed her eyes and relished the silence.

Seven days of family and food, neighbors and guests, prayers and songs piled upon scant sleep had exhausted Elizabeth. With all the commotion, an outsider seeing this joyful old couple would have thought they were hosting a wedding banquet for their child, not welcoming their newborn. Today she rested, but tomorrow the guests would come again, not only to celebrate but also for the naming ceremony and the baby's circumcision.

It was tradition. Eight days after birth infants were ceremoniously named, and boys were marked with the sign of circumcision, an outward reminder of God's covenant with his people.

Elizabeth had heard them discussing the baby's name but had been too tired to alert them that the job had already been done.

Months ago, Zechariah had been stirring coals into the fire with a stick. He stopped suddenly and clapped his hands for her attention. She hurried to his side.

Zechariah pointed his smoldering stirring stick toward the fire. There in the ash, with the charred end of his stick, Zechariah had written Hebrew letters. She recognized it as Hebrew writing—some word—but she had never learned to read it.

She looked from the writing to Zechariah and shrugged.

He retraced the letters, searched her for some trace of understanding, but she could give none. She pointed to the fire and slowly mouthed syllables to him. Fire?

He shook his head.

Hot? That wasn't it.

Black? She ventured, seeing the burned chunks of wood.

He hung his head, tossed the stick into the dying fire and went to bed.

The next morning a neighbor and her son stopped by

and offered to fetch the water for Elizabeth. The woman's young son, on his way to synagogue, followed her inside and wandered around the room. As Elizabeth thanked her friend and handed her the water jar, she noticed the young boy studying the charred letters in last night's ash. He quietly drew out the sounds, "Jaaw-nnn."

His mother took the jar from Elizabeth, called him to come along, and they were off again.

Elizabeth returned to the ash. The black letters were still there.

Zechariah sat praying near the window. She knelt, laid a hand on his knee, and he opened his eyes. On eye level with him, she pointed to the writing and said "John."

He nodded with a grateful smile, took her face in his hands, and kissed her forehead.

She gave Zechariah's knee a satisfied squeeze.

The baby wriggled on her shoulder as if participating in his infant dream.

"John," She whispered, and he settled. *John.* She liked it.

But she knew the family coming tomorrow would not. "Oh, Lord," she prayed, "You have given us this son, and you have decided his name. Help me tomorrow to proclaim what you have declared."

Is there anything too hard for the Lord? He will grant what he requires.

Righteous and blameless as he was, Zechariah knew what the child must be named, and though the Bible does not detail how he communicated this to Elizabeth, somehow, when the time came, she was certain. "His name is John" (Luke 1:60, NLT).

Perhaps because Zechariah's first act of unbelief had cost him a memorable price, he was determined to obey God and let Elizabeth know what God had said.

It was such an apt name. The name *John* means, "God is gracious."

God was gracious to discipline Zechariah and not let him remain in a state of skepticism and unbelief.

God was gracious to give him the boundary of speechlessness, lest he say something else he'd regret. God provided forty weeks of undistracted days to speak to God only in his mind and listen to God's voice alone. God was the only one he could effortlessly converse with. The judgement of silence was also the gracious gift that propelled him towards belief and obedience to God in the future.

God was gracious to remove the "reproach" of childlessness from their home. In a sense, God had vindicated them. The blessing of this son smothered rumors that their childless home was a consequence of secret sin.

God was gracious to communicate to Elizabeth the name he chose for their boy, and somehow, he did it without a word from Zechariah.

God's grand story is headed somewhere definite, and along the way, his aim is to reveal himself to the people he loves and rescue them from sin.

His purposes remain the same, and he is still graciously fulfilling them.

When we make a practice of sin, his strong hand lifting our chins to meet his gaze feels shameful. *I'm sorry. I knew better. I couldn't stop.* Red-faced and crying, we have the urge to turn from him and cover up. We blame, make reasonable excuses, and justify ourselves. But God is gracious. If we confess, he will forgive (1 John 1:9). Can we view his loving discipline as a facet of his grace?

What happens when we ask him for a spouse, a child, or a restored relationship, but in the darkness of the present situation we can't make out a single ray of hope? "Darkness is as light to you," said the psalmist (Psalm 139:12). God can see clearly as if it were noon. We can trust that even in the pitch-black darkness God is not fumbling his way forward. His wide-eyed guidance, and the Psalms that tell us about it, are also gifts of his grace.

"Your path led through the sea," wrote the psalmist, "your way through the mighty waters, though your footprints were not seen" (Psalm 77:19). Where God calls us to go, he will make a path. It might be through mighty waters or the stilted conversations of believers, but he has already laid plans to part the sea and communicate through a mute man.

Often, we cannot see God's footprints—the concrete evidence of his presence and leading. But the end results point directly to his gracious leading, even when we can't explain exactly how he got us through.

God is gracious, indeed.

Oh, Lord,

Thank you for somehow providing a way for a mute old man to communicate with his illiterate wife. No plan of yours can be thwarted, and your provision never stops. Though the mighty sea rolls back together to hide your footprints, remind us you were with us each step of the way.

Zechariah's Blessing

Then they made signs to his father, to find out what he would like to name the child. He asked for a writing tablet, and to everyone's astonishment he wrote, "His name is John." Immediately his mouth was opened and his tongue set free, and he began to speak, praising God.

—Luke 1:62-64

It was going to be a big day for Zechariah's little family. The baby would receive his name and the covenant sign of circumcision, declaring him one of God's chosen people. But Zechariah knew God had already named and chosen him long ago.

Mary stood near the front door and welcomed the neighbors and relatives arriving to celebrate and witness.

As Zechariah watched their guests file in, he counted them. Ten witnesses would satisfy the requirements of the law, and they were well beyond that now.

Traditionally, Zechariah would have had the honor of performing the ceremony. But because he could not speak, his cousin, who served with him as a priest, would have the privilege instead.

Disappointed as he was, it was clear to Zechariah that God's plan was in full swing, and nine months of silence had given him plenty of time to consider what it meant to take God at his word.

There was so much to be said, and yet he couldn't speak. Here they were, on the eve of a new era for Israel, and Zechariah alone knew all the angel's words. God would ready his people to receive the Saving King he had promised so many years ago. Israel would finally be free from centuries of political turbulence, wars, and illegitimate kings.

The good news bubbled inside him like a kettle over the fire. And yet, his lid was latched, and he could not speak of it.

Everyone was in place. His cousin, the priest, began the ceremony by lifting his hands to God in prayer. As Zechariah had done so many times for other families in their town, his cousin recited the benediction. His lips moved quickly through memorized words, and his beard bobbed up and down with each syllable.

Zechariah had arranged all the ceremonial necessities

on the table. Water rippled in the bowl, and a linen tow-el lay folded beside it. The curved handle and blade of a flint knife wobbled each time the table was bumped. There was a goblet of wine for Elizabeth and him to drink in celebration of the completed ceremony, and each item waited for its turn.

Elizabeth handed the baby to the priest. He prayed again as he placed the naked, and now wriggling, baby in the lap of his assistant. The baby's cheeks reddened, and he opened his mouth in painful protest. Zechariah felt a sympathetic shudder run up his spine. As the baby lay on his back, tiny tears ran from the corners of his eyes into his ears. The assistant dressed the wound, swaddled the baby, and handed him to Elizabeth who nursed him back to calm.

As his head was nestled in the crook of his mother's arm, Zechariah had wanted to whisper in his ear, *You are chosen by God.* Instead, he stroked the baby's head.

The priest traded the cup of wine for the baby. Elizabeth drank and handed the cup to Zechariah. As the priest's mouth formed the words of the familiar naming prayer, "And let his name be called in Israel," Zechariah watched for one word as he continued "Zachariah, the son of Zachariah. Let his father rejoice..."

Elizabeth elbowed him, and he realized she had de-cided to interrupt the prayer. She shook her head, and he saw her say, "No. His name is John."

Zechariah smiled, and she returned a nod.

He knew they wouldn't like it. At his age, he had fewer years left than he had already lived. Of course, they wanted the baby to carry his name to the next generation. But this child's job would be to carry another name and another message. And each of these unforgettable events would have them talking and looking for the Messiah.

Frowning, the priest argued with Elizabeth and pointed to Zechariah. Tradition demanded a family name. Neighbors turned to whisper to one another, no doubt suggesting other well-known family names.

He wanted to chuckle at all their disgruntled faces. The dissatisfied group turned to him with questioning expressions. They held the baby up to his face as if he'd gone blind instead of deaf. Gesturing with indignation, the group seemed to be asking, *What on earth is Elizabeth talking about?* And, *What do you want to name him?*

Zechariah motioned toward his cousin's satchel on the floor and pretended to write on his own hand. They understood and brought him a wooden plank lightly coated with wax. With the stylus, he carved these words: His name is John.

He held out the writing to his cousin and saw him read it aloud. Confusion replaced their worried irritation. The hyped emotion of a moment ago drained from their faces.

And he had to laugh.

What was that? He heard himself laughing.

Elizabeth's sweet voice rushed into his ears like fresh

breeze through pines. She was saying, "I know there's no one in our family called John, but that is his name. God has given it."

Zechariah was overcome with emotion.

He slid from his chair to the floor, and on bended knee, raised his hands and voice to heaven. The long-silenced blessing, the swelling praise, and the angel's message erupted, and he began to speak in broken sobs:

"Praise the Lord, the God of Israel, because he has visited and redeemed his people" (Luke 1:68, NLT).

Every chattering guest hushed and turned toward the frail father worshiping out loud. With his audience in stunned silence, he declared the news at last.

"He has sent us a mighty Savior from the royal line of his servant David, just as he promised through his holy prophets long ago. Now we will be saved from our enemies and from all who hate us. He has been merciful to our ancestors by remembering his sacred covenant—the covenant he swore with an oath to our ancestor Abraham. We have been rescued from our enemies so we can serve God without fear, in holiness and righteousness for as long as we live" (Luke 1:69-75, NLT).

Zechariah supported himself on the chair and stood. Elizabeth held baby John and wiped a tear with her sleeve. With one hand on her shoulder and one on their son, Zechariah leaned over them both. Tears rolled down his cheeks and splashed on the blanket as Zechariah blessed his son.

"And you, my little son will be called the prophet of the Most High, because you will prepare the way for the Lord (Luke 1:76, NLT).

Zechariah looked around the room, his face imploring them all to believe. He kissed John's head and spoke in a reverent tone: "You will tell his people how to find salvation through forgiveness of their sins. Because of God's tender mercy, the morning light from heaven is about to break upon us, to give light to those who sit in darkness and in the shadow of death, and to guide us to the path of peace" (Luke 1:77-79, NLT).

Zechariah bowed his head, thanked God silently— this time by choice—for the blessings of promise and fulfillment, silence and speech.

৯৫

Ten months of delayed obedience.

That's what doubt does. It delays obedience. And if allowed to continue, doubt stops obedience altogether.

When God applied his gracious intervention of discipline, Zechariah's doubtful skepticism was transformed into a worship song of absolute certainty—as sure as the sun rises.

His son's name would be like an Old Testament standing stone–a means to remember–like those rocks once pulled from the Jordan River when Israel crossed on dry land. In obedience, Israel's leaders had arranged them as a monument. When their children asked, "What are these stones for?" (See Joshua 4:21), they could recount the miraculous work of God.

How gracious of God to command Zechariah and Elizabeth to set a sign of remembrance on their son—his name. So whenever someone asked, "Why did you name him John? There's no one in your family named John," Zechariah and Elizabeth could recount the work of their miraculous God and declare, "We named him John because God is gracious."

Dear Lord,

Give us a heart like Zechariah's. One that accepts due discipline as a great grace. One that endures discipline and learns to trust. One that has no response but praise when it has finally learned what you have taught.

Talk of the Town

All the neighbors were filled with awe, and throughout the hill country of Judea people were talking about all these things. Everyone who heard this wondered about it, asking, "What then is this child going to be?" For the Lord's hand was with him.

—Luke 1:65-66

Mary dipped the towel from the ceremony into her washbasin. She scrubbed smudges of blood with a piece of soap, then plunged it into the basin again to rinse. The priest had cleared their table and stuffed his satchel with the clean goblet, his writing tablet and, of course, the knife. In their place, neighbors had deposited loaves of barley bread and cheese rounds wrapped in cloth. One woman gave a basket of eggs with a leafy grape vine festively wound around the handle. Mary scooted it away from the edge and toward the middle of the table. She didn't need a mess of raw eggs splattered on the floor.

Neighbors had been so generous to Zechariah and Elizabeth. It was an oddity to behold—a new life from old ones—but they gladly worshiped and rejoiced. They spoke of Abraham and Sarah, who were also given a child when their energy for childrearing was long gone. As Mary had moved among the guests, she'd heard one ask, "What do you suppose this little child, John, might become since he's arrived in the manner of our patriarch Isaac?"

They were right to wonder. His conception, birth and his father's unexplained speechlessness were regularly discussed as young mothers fetched water for their families. Men, old and young, argued reasons for the old priest's predicament. He had been unexplainably childless and speechless. For nearly a year, Zechariah hadn't spoken to any of them. And then, as God had stopped the Jordan river, he unleashed it, and Zechariah burst into praise and thanksgiving.

They were right to wonder.

As Mary tossed the dirty water outside, a neighbor hurried past and waved to a man on the road. The traveler stopped and Mary saw two friends catching up on all that had passed between them.

"Where're you headed?" the neighbor asked his traveling friend.

"Back to Jerusalem," he replied. "What's the news here in the hill country?"

"You'll hardly believe it when I tell you," he smiled. "Remember Zechariah, the old priest?"

"Of course," the traveler replied. "Zechariah and Elizabeth, of the tribe of Aaron?"

"That's right." He nodded with glee over what he was about to report. "God gave them a son."

Mary watched the traveler's face contort. Tipping his head and raising an eyebrow, he tried to distinguish if his long-time friend was joking, lying, intoxicated, or if he himself had misunderstood. "They've adopted a son to care for them as they age?"

"No," he insisted, "Elizabeth has given him a baby."

Still confused, the traveler asked, "I'd heard Zechariah wasn't well. Unable to speak, I thought. But I haven't seen him for months. Probably since he was last in Jerusalem."

The neighbor recounted the entire story, as told by Zechariah to everyone attending the ceremony the previous day. He included all the most astonishing details: God's angelic messenger, Gabriel; a baby for the aged couple; the immediate judgement for Zechariah's doubting unbelief; and finally, the God-given name.

"John? There's no one in their family named John." The traveler interrupted.

"You're right, but that's not the most incredible part. Zechariah is no longer mute, and he has prophesied that God has visited us and is sending the King."

"You can't mean Herod." Mary felt sorry for the traveler. It sounded so unusual now as she heard it retold.

"No! Not Herod." He looked around, as if someone might pounce. "The Messiah," he whispered.

Still unsure the traveler conceded, "Well, he can't come soon enough."

"Zechariah speaks as if he's on his way."

"Who is it then? Zechariah's son?" He raised a skeptical eyebrow.

"No ... but Zechariah says the Messiah is coming."

Slowly, they had moved down the road together and were out of earshot now. Mary stepped back into the house, closed the door, and leaned up against it. On the other side of the room, Elizabeth rocked John while Zechariah hummed a psalm. Permanent smiles pushed sagging skin upward on their sleepy faces.

And Mary's thoughts returned to the roadside report. News would spread like pollen in spring and dust the hills all the way to Jerusalem. In her lifetime, the Messiah would declare his Kingship. Mary closed her heavy eyelids and smiled too. She placed her hand on her growing tummy.

You can be sure, he's definitely on his way.

৯৳

Though they were all regular people, there was nothing ordinary about the way God was moving in Zechariah, Elizabeth, Mary and the chattering villagers in and around Jerusalem. God was speaking to his people again. Sending messages via angels and even through disciplined servants, like Zechariah. Everyone who heard about it turned it to examine every angle in bewilderment, as though a multifaceted gem had been dug from their back yard.

The miracles of God sometimes come like his word, with two sharp edges.

First there is the undeniable answered prayer. A healing, a pregnancy, a deliverance of some sort. Each circumstance brought about by undeniable divine intervention. There is happiness over the healing, joy over the child, and corporate gratitude for what God has done.

But after the miracle settles in, the baby is born, life returns to normal rhythms, the second edge of that sword flashes in the light as friends and family, neighbors and strangers make the recipient of the miracle the talk of their evening meals and the subject of their visiting walks.

And while it is encouraging to remember the uncommon, in our humanity we are too quick to turn our eye from the Miracle Worker to examine the miracle's recipient.

Elizabeth and Zechariah and baby John were discussed around the dinner tables of Judea. While Zechariah and Elizabeth rejoiced, the whole town rehashed their long story.

And when folks are whispering about others, they are also withdrawing from them. It is awkward to have talked about the private events of someone else's life at supper and then to meet them face-to-face the next morning on your way to work.

With the joy of divine intervention there is sometimes the pain of isolation, as Mary would soon find out.

But God has never initiated a circumstance he couldn't redeem.

While all the hill country of Judea chatted about the particulars, Zechariah and Elizabeth lived them. They taught John the whole story and lived what they'd learned right in front of their little boy. In doing so, they prepared the boy who would prepare the way for the King.

Oh, Lord,

When you begin a work the reverberations of your movement resonates in the hearts of all who are called according to your purpose. Even in isolating obedience, you are with us to complete your work. Thank you for working in fragile people.

Nazareth Awaits

Mary stayed with Elizabeth for about three
months and then returned home.

—Luke 1:56

Mary unfolded the same square of fabric she had used
to pack belongings three months earlier. The time had
passed at a frightful pace. Perhaps it was the school of
pregnancy and motherhood that caused the days to fly.
Mary would have feared for her baby's life if Elizabeth
hadn't assured her the pain in her back meant she needed to drink more water. And after working alongside
Elizabeth's midwife, the delivery and the proper care of a
newborn were fresh in Mary's mind.

But maybe the days had flown by because she knew
she must eventually return to Nazareth. The caravan she
had traveled with was headed north again. She planned
to join them and return to her town, her synagogue, her

home, her parents, and her soon-to-be husband.

But nothing would be the same.

"Oh, good, you haven't tied up your bundle yet." Elizabeth had stepped into the room without Mary's notice. "I've wrapped some food for you to take."

"Oh, Elizabeth. You ought to keep it. The neighbors brought it for you."

"I know. They've been so generous. But by the time we eat everything else, these loaves will be furry with mold."

Mary knew she was right. The table was still stacked with edible gifts. Bread was light enough to carry and already cooked, but her appetite had been sporadic since she'd arrived. One morning she'd wake wishing she could eat an entire loaf with honey and a cup full of almonds. The next day she'd be sick at the smell of it.

"Thank you," Mary said.

"As the baby grows, you'll feel more like eating. Oh..." Elizabeth rushed back to the kitchen, "I meant to send a little salt and olive oil, too."

She'd get hungry sooner or later, but she didn't feel like eating just now.

Her growing tummy was still mostly hidden under her roomy tunic, but the place where she usually knotted her belt was several inches too small now. She loosened the knot and tied it higher on her waist.

There was no hiding it. She had accepted this great privilege, but she knew it would be difficult to explain. Unbelievable, actually.

Poor Joseph. She'd known him for as long as she could remember. With the other children in Nazareth they'd thrown rocks in the spring, chased lambs into the corral, and dragged sticks through the dirt to mark their path. He was a neighbor and a friend.

But they were older now. Her father had met with Joseph's. In a matter of months, they were no longer merely neighbors and friends. She and Joseph were betrothed—pledged to one another for marriage within the next year.

He was a good man and she was thankful. Other girls hadn't been as fortunate.

Joseph was a young but skilled carpenter, and the room he was preparing for them must be nearly completed by now. She was anxious to see it, eager to be married, but terribly concerned.

In the old days they would have stoned her, innocent or not. Of course, she was not an adulterer. God knew it. She knew it. Even Elizabeth knew it. But if God did not intervene on her behalf, and on behalf of his son, serious consequences awaited her in Nazareth.

Elizabeth returned with a knotted ball of linen in her hand. "It's the oil. The stopper is secure, but you'd hate to have it break in your pack. You can give it to your mother as a gift from me if there's any left when you arrive."

Mary burst into tears and buried her face in Elizabeth's chest, the cushioned bottle of oil sandwiched between them. "How will I explain when I get there?"

she whispered.

Elizabeth stroked her hair and answered, "God goes before you, Mary. He's already been there. You remember the song of David?" and Elizabeth sang the familiar words to Mary.

"You have searched me, Lord, and you know me.

You know when I sit and when I rise; you perceive my thoughts from afar."

Mary, with quivering voice, joined her in the next lines. "You hem me in behind and before, and you lay your hand upon me."

Elizabeth put her hands on both sides of Mary's face, and reassured her. "Remember God's message to you, Mary."

Mary nodded and the angel's comforting words echoed again bringing calm relief.

Nothing is impossible with God.

Mary was highly favored, chosen, and still she was human.

Even a highly favored woman with a divine calling of bearing God's son would have been, like you and me, prone to worry ... or at least wonder.

But for Mary, the miracle, God's plan, was already in progress. She had placed herself under the gracious hand of her unimaginably wild God. By God's good design there was, for Mary, no turning back.

The baby grew, and so did Mary's tummy. Every day was a confirmation of God's unfolding promise to rescue his people through One Perfect King.

The synagogue leaders in that day taught that the Messiah would be more angelic than human, more divine than earthly. This kind of teaching painted pictures of him coming in the clouds of heaven. Perhaps this is one reason they did not recognize or receive him (See John 1:11). They were looking into the sky, and he was already being knit together on earth.

Imagine the contradiction and the questioning when all Mary had been taught bumped into what she had experienced by the overshadowing of the Holy Spirit. Amid such a quandary, she must have asked the Lord at least one more time in the privacy of her own heart, "How will this be?"

Over and over she must have leaned on the angel's strong and wide-open comfort. "Nothing is impossible with God."

It is even possible for unknown people in unrecognized places with unpopular surroundings to participate in God's grand and unfolding plan.

Brace yourself, obscure one, for nothing is impossible with God.

۶

Oh, Lord,

You never said obedience would be easy. We are eager when you speak and tenuous when months separate us from your call. Help us to trust your words no matter how long it's been since we first heard or read them.

A Hardworking Husband

This is how the birth of Jesus Christ came about: His mother Mary was pledged to be married to Joseph...

—Matthew 1:18

Joseph was sweating to the cadence of his rising and falling saw. With the room finished, he planned to build a couple of small pieces of furniture for Mary.

He sawed through the fourth length of a table leg, and it dropped at his feet. He couldn't afford furniture for their home, but with everything he'd learned from his father, he could build it instead. And all that experience was serving him well.

For the past year Joseph had been preparing for the day he would bring Mary home as his wife. He had known her since they were small, but in the past several years he began to notice her.

His father and hers had met on several occasions, none of which interested Joseph, initially. But after her father brought Mary to the house, Joseph started paying attention.

A year ago, they had made it official. The betrothal ceremony was short and simple. With the exchange of gifts and words, they were legally bound by promises.

Much had happened since then. Joseph began building a room onto his father's house which would be his and Mary's. Their own room. At first, it was awkward thinking of Mary as his wife. As he laid their foundation stones, raised walls to shield them from cold and heat, and built a roof to cover their home, he'd begun calling it "our place." A year later, he could hardly imagine living there without her. With the job nearly finished, he'd proven himself a faithful and worthy husband.

He eyed the cut stone and framed window. It was no palace, but Mary would not complain. They'd spent their whole lives in this tiny town, and no one they knew was accustomed to luxury. Mary was not the demanding sort. She was helpful and kind.

She'd proven it again several months ago when she left Nazareth in a hurry to help her elderly cousin, Elizabeth. It was unusual, Joseph thought, to see Mary rushing off with a caravan. She seemed distracted and concerned for Elizabeth. But her father had allowed it, and in deference to her father, Joseph had not protested. Mary was a girl who respected and cared for people, so he shouldn't think it out of character.

Joseph sanded splinters off each leg of the table and then tapped them into place so he could turn the piece upright. The top was adorned with the natural wonders of wood that he loved to admire. Tree knots and woodgrain were God's design. Slicing them open to discover what God had done was one of Joseph's greatest pleasure. The fragrance of fresh cedar and finishing oil combined to make a kind of incense that rose to heaven with Joseph's gratitude. "Thank you, God, for this privilege." It wasn't elaborate, but it wasn't common either. Mary's approving smile would be worth the work.

He expected her return any day. Their wedding was approaching fast, and he was eager to show her all he had done. Things had gone so smoothly, and he was sure the table would be a pleasant surprise.

Joseph was a righteous man as we discover in the next verses of our passage (See Matthew 1:19). Just as in the case of Zechariah and Elizabeth, "righteous," does not mean he lived without sin. But it does mean that Joseph was careful and mindful of honoring God and obeying his laws.

For a man of his age and stage in life, being righteous

meant working hard at a trade, most likely the one his father had taught him. It meant paying careful attention to honoring his parents, even as an adult. Arranged marriages in the Jewish culture were their standard and tradition, and as a righteous man, Joseph deferred to his father's choice for him.

Being engaged to Mary meant preparing a place to live, with space for their family to grow, and a home where God would be honored.

For such a man we might expect God to smile upon Joseph with all the blessings we would prefer for ourselves. We'd hope that a man like Joseph lived a long and satisfying life, but most scholars believe Joseph died years before Jesus did. We want to rest assured that a righteous and diligent father like Joseph would never experience the panic of losing a child for three days in a crowded capital city. And wouldn't it be God's will to grant Joseph a son who would grow up to be a man whom religious leaders could respect?

But we cannot earn or dictate what blessings God ought to bestow, and those were not the blessings Joseph received.

Joseph was about to be leveled by God's favor in ways he could never have imagined.

We fall into a sticky trap of disappointment when we expect to earn specific favors from God, but we are so prone to that kind of thinking. We're predisposed to living as though we can and must earn God's favor and blessing. We are sometimes motivated to obey God in order to get what we expect from him.

If I work hard, God owes me financial success.

If I marry a believer, God owes me a blissful marriage.

If I take my family to church, God owes me a happy family.

Sounds kind of ugly when it's stated like that, but it's a very subtle way we try to direct God's actions.

Our responsibility is not to put God in our service, but to place ourselves under the orchestration of his plan and let him direct our actions. He is eager to bless his children according to his will, but sometimes it means a wild and unexplainable ride we never anticipated.

❧

Dear Lord,

Thank you for the times in life when things are sailing smoothly. It is rest for our minds and a gift from you. Though we are less inclined to lean into you when we have few reasons, help us remember you are good and sovereign in the smooth sailing as well as in the storm.

A Tough Day

...but before they came together, she was found
to be pregnant through the Holy Spirit.

—Matthew 1:18

The sound of skillful hammering came from behind the
house. *He's home.*

Mary knocked on the door of Joseph's father's home,
hoping they could hear her above the noise. Her visit
would be unexpected and possibly unwelcome. She was
painfully aware of that. But Elizabeth had encouraged
her to speak with Joseph before their wedding, and Mary
wanted to heed her cousin's advice.

She brought a gift of braided bread for Joseph and his
family. A peace offering of sorts.

Joseph's father came to the door and, without a welcome, hollered for Joseph.

Sweaty, winded, and handsome, Joseph appeared at

the door, still holding the hammer. Mary remembered the bread and handed it to Joseph's father.

"I made it this morning." She forced a smile.

He turned to take it to his wife and left them in the doorway alone.

Joseph's whole face spoke of relief at her return, but Mary knew there was no time for pleasantries. She spoke softly. "There's something I must tell you."

Her voice was calm, but her words clearly stirred his nerves.

He raised an eyebrow and smiled out of one side of his mouth. "What?"

"Joseph, I'm going to have a baby."

He dropped the hammer, and all that pleasant relief drained from his face.

"But you must know I have not been unfaithful to you, Joseph. This baby is from the Holy Spirit." She hurried to explain about the angel, his good news, Elizabeth's confirmation.

But Joseph was speechless.

Joseph's father appeared in the door again, and she knew it was time for her to leave. "Thank you for the bread, Mary. You will make a good wife for Joseph." He smiled and slapped his bewildered son on the shoulder.

"Thank you," Mary replied and turned to go.

The pounding at the back of the house resumed as she walked toward home. But the skillful hammering she heard on her arrival turned fierce and erratic on her departure.

Mary shivered.

God had brought her this far. He would bring her far-
ther. With or without Joseph.

❧

Though Mary didn't know it yet, her heart was already
being pierced by the blessing of being the mother of
the Messiah. God had not promised her a husband, or
a house, or a long life. The angel mentioned nothing
about Joseph.

If Mary was highly favored, and if the Lord was with
her, as the angel said, then it seems like God might be
obliged to give her a reasonably stress-free and comfortable life.

But he didn't.

It wouldn't be a stretch to say Mary was batted around
by a most unpredictable and terrifying string of stress-
ors. Within the next year she traveled seventy miles, on
foot, to Bethlehem, then several more miles, on foot, carrying a newborn to Jerusalem. Months later, they fled
Bethlehem. The screams of bereaved mothers chased
them to the foreign soil of Egypt, a place known as the
land of Israel's captivity. Later, God gave Joseph a dream
that would rescue them from refugee status by promising

it was safe to return to Israel. Years after they first left Nazareth, they packed up and settled in their hometown. There, they raised a full house of children—Jesus and the other babies that came along every couple of years. Because gospel writers don't mention Joseph beyond the childhood of Jesus, it's likely Mary was a widowed single mother at some point. She witnessed the crucifixion of God's Son—her innocent son—for sins and crimes he did not commit. As she sobbed near his cross, she was placed in the care of her son's friend John.

Her life circumstances, distilled and summarized, don't sound like blessings anyone would choose.

But all this demonstrates the transformative power of God's call on a person's life. When God undeniably calls you to a task, your readiness is quick, your willingness is eager, and your certainty may cause you to appear plain crazy. But several decades after Mary was found to be with child, she could be found in an upper room in Jerusalem gathered with believers, waiting for the promised Holy Spirit (See Acts 1:14).

Years later, the apostle Paul would write, "I am not ashamed of the gospel, because it is the power of God that brings salvation to everyone who believes," (Romans 1:16). The irrevocable call of God still has the same power in the lives of believers who say, "I am the Lord's servant." Although we declare our allegiance without knowing how it will all pan out, we have this certainty, from Jesus: "I will ask the Father, and he will give you another advocate to help you and be with you forever—the Spirit of truth. The world cannot accept him, because it neither sees him nor knows him. But you know him, for he lives with you and will be in you" (John 14:16-17).

His promise still stands.

※

Oh, Lord,

We are shaken when you interrupt our well-laid plans. Help us remember your ways are not our ways, neither are they an interruption. In fact, they are the only purposes worth pursuing. Thank you for keeping your promise to be ever present with us.

Day 16

A Righteous Man

Because Joseph her husband was faithful to the
law, and yet did not want to expose her to public
disgrace, he had in mind to divorce her quietly.

—Matthew 1:19

Joseph thought he would scream or be sick. He pound-
ed away at the table to redirect his raging emotions. He
wanted to destroy the furniture rather than finish it. But
that would only alarm his family and unleash a string of
disgraceful events.

He was astounded. Had he been duped? Was he so
foolish to think this adulterer was kind?

She offered no apology. No remorse. Just a plain declaration, as if she were telling him a meal was ready.

His anger and absolute disbelief were soon joined by
deep sadness and regret. He threw his hammer into the
dirt and turned the table upright. Unwilling to expend

any more effort on an unwanted gift, he sat on it.

Adultery.

Even if Mary wasn't willing to abide by God's laws, he would. He knew what God's law required. He kicked the scrap wood at his feet and considered his miserable options.

Her actions would be an embarrassment to her family, to his, and to both of them individually. If he insisted on public discipline, as was his right, both of their families would be dragged through the mud, but Mary would suffer the brunt of it. And though he was angry and bewildered, he could not bear the thought of her public humiliation.

I've got to get out of here.

Joseph wanted to be alone—to run far from this room and this table and every reminder that his work and preparation had been wasted. But just as he stood to get some distance from the monuments of poor judgment, his father called the family to eat.

Joseph couldn't stomach a bite, but he was the first to be offered Mary's braided loaf. He hesitated and his father laughed, "Come on now, she isn't trying to poison you."

Joseph forced a smile. He hadn't even considered that. Until now.

On any other day Joseph was sure he could have survived a month on her bread alone. Mary made it, after all. But now that fact made it crumbly and tasteless. And while his family swooned over her handiwork, he had to refrain from spitting it out.

"Another piece?" His mother held out the loaf for him to tear off another share.

"No, thanks." He got up from the table and went outside.

The dark canopy of the night sky was pocked with holes, as if all the sun's brightness was stored on the other side. A pigeon cooed somewhere under an eave. Windows glowed with the light of small oil lamps set on tables or ledges indoors. In one house, a child whined, and its mother's muffled scolding tumbled out the window. He passed a fenced flock of sheep and startled them. Scampering in circles around their pen, they were as confused as he was. It had seemed a good match. He rehashed childhood interactions with her and their grown-up conversations. Not one memory would yield a warning he should have heeded. With his hands in his pockets, he'd been socked in the face.

The evening passed without him realizing it, and he arrived at his front door again. The oil lamps had been extinguished and he was glad he wouldn't see his father. Joseph felt foolish and knew his father would too, so Joseph made plans to salve the shame.

Early tomorrow morning, before the synagogue was busy, he would go and obtain a certificate of divorce. It was unlawful to marry an adulterer, and even though Mary's sin angered him, it fortified his commitment to the law. God's seventh commandment said, "You shall not commit adultery" (Exodus 20:14). And he wouldn't. He knew what must be done.

But he was also heartbroken. His work on the house and the little table could no longer be a gift. Instead they would be a daily reminder of unfaithfulness. He would work within those walls where he had imagined their life together, and every stone would remind him of broken promises.

Beyond that, he was concerned for Mary and her outrageous claims. An angel? A baby by the Holy Spirit? The Son of God? Not only was it irrational, it seemed dangerously close to blasphemy.

She would have enough difficulty in Nazareth bearing and raising a child without a husband. He hoped she would keep her story to herself before something much worse than adultery or divorce came upon her.

Joseph quietly latched the door and felt his way in the dark toward his bed. He rolled on top, not caring to pull back the blankets. His mind churned. His heart ached. The walk had not helped. His body was restless and yet weighed down with fatigue and grief. Sunrise was only a few hours away.

God, give me rest so I can honor you with a clear mind tomorrow.

And within minutes he felt himself sinking into the sweet relief of sleep.

❧

For all his righteousness, hard work, and waiting, Joseph was rewarded with an announcement of what appeared to be scandalous infidelity.

His girl was pregnant.

According to God's laws, which he tried to obey, marrying an unfaithful woman would make him unfaithful too. So, to avoid further disgracing his family and Mary's, he meant to break it off quietly. He'd swallow the embarrassment, follow God's law, and endure a heartbreaking obedience—a disturbing reversal that would not go unnoticed.

In the face of what appeared to be an epic betrayal, Joseph was anchored by God's word and carried along by God's compassion. It would have been inconsistent with his upright character to cast Mary, vulnerable as she was, into the public eye to be the subject of a hundred disgusted dinnertime conversations. But no matter how quietly it was done, in a small town like Nazareth, the whispers would be loud.

Difficult obedience sometimes appears to make a mess of things.

In that same synagogue in Nazareth where Joseph was headed to quietly obey God, just thirty short years later, Jesus would stand and read from Isaiah. He would announce that he himself was the Promised One who would give a crown of beauty in exchange for the ashes of grief, and the oil of gladness in exchange for mourning. His obedience would also make a mess of things there in his hometown.

Sometimes God's blessings begin in the most unlikely and unwanted ways. Ruinous circumstances. Life-altering events. People who upend our lives. And none of it feels like blessing at the outset.

With the ashes of well-laid plans scattered at our feet, we may be inclined to run away from the mess or shake our fists at God for ruining things with his hard commands.

But our job is not to reassemble the pieces. Our job is to do what he asks. We can present to God the unmet expectations, the betrayal, the sadness, and the whole slew of emotional debris, and let him do what he does best.

In the middle of a smoldering mess, God can give a crown of beauty in exchange for our ashes of grief. It doesn't always happen overnight. But sometimes it does.

Oh, Lord,

To one teenager you announce immediate good news. To the other you allowed a period of devastating grief. Even in their grieving the loss of the other, they still sought to obey.

When we discover that our plans are not yours, help us to obey you without compromise, even in the face of great disappointment.

Joseph Gets the Message

But after he had considered this, an angel of the Lord appeared to him in a dream and said, "Joseph son of David, do not be afraid to take Mary home as your wife, because what is conceived in her is from the Holy Spirit. She will give birth to a son, and you are to give him the name Jesus, because he will save his people from their sins."

—Matthew 1:20-21

Joseph heard his name and feared he had slept too long. His opportunity to escape to the synagogue in solitude was over. From behind closed eyelids he could see light.

"Joseph, son of David." He heard it again.

Joseph opened his eyes with a start. Out his window the sky was still dark, but his room was not. He shook his head to clear the confusion.

There, at the foot of his bed, stood a shining light. Not a lamp, but not a man. Joseph was unable to speak or swallow. He lay there, as if pinned, motionless except the painful throbbing of his heart.

Then it, or he, stepped around the corner of Joseph's bed. Terror broke the invisible force holding Joseph down, and he scrambled backward until his back hit the wall and held him there. Brightness forced Joseph to close his eyes again. *God in heaven,* he began to pray silently.

"Joseph."

He was startled back to wide-eyed fright.

"Do not be afraid to take Mary home as your wife."

Had the raging regrets of last night followed him in sleep? Joseph rubbed his eyes and raked his fingers through his hair to force upon himself the reality that he was truly awake and there was, indeed, an angel speaking to him.

"Mary tells you the truth," the angel continued. "She is pregnant. But she is not an adulterer because the baby conceived in her is from the Holy Spirit."

Mary's confession rang in his head, now accompanied by this heavenly declaration. *An angel. A baby by the Holy Spirit.*

"She will give birth to a son. And you, Joseph, are to name him Jesus—'God Saves'—because he will save his people from their sins."

The Messiah?

As quickly as the angel had appeared, he was gone.

Joseph's mouth was dry, and he still could not swallow. He heard panting and realized it was his own. Exhaustion knocked him out and he felt unable to keep his eyes open.

When Joseph woke again, sunlight streamed through the window, and he was alone. Morning had come, and he had no divorce papers.

He stared at the foot of the bed where an angel had stood. Were those footprints in the dust? In that sacred place between sleep and wakefulness, an angel's words were seared into his mind—a holy announcement binding up all his unraveling plans.

Joseph stood to get dressed for the day and realized he hadn't undressed the night before. His tangled hair and wrinkled tunic did not even warrant a hesitation. He rushed through the house and out the door.

Mary was not an adulterer. She was graced by God to mother the promised King. And he would belong to Joseph's distant, but royal, family heritage.

She was not an insane blasphemer. She was obedient and honest.

And the angel had said to *marry,* not divorce.

Joseph hurried through the street toward Mary's father's house, once again startling the penned sheep as he passed. *Of all the people, and all the places,* Joseph marveled. *Why me? Why Mary? Why Nazareth?* So much uncertainty clouded his mind. But one thing he knew for sure, he would obey God's messenger. He would take Mary as his wife.

And in obedience, they would raise God's Son and name him Jesus.

❧

Imagine the emotional anguish roiling in Joseph's head and heart as he wrestled with what to do. Every activity of the past year was aimed toward a lifetime with Mary.

Then came the devastating shock. The proverbial two-by-four upside the head that sent him spinning. A baby by the Holy Spirit.

While reeling in the aftershocks of such an emotional earthquake, Joseph turned to steady himself on his immovable God of whom David had written, "The Lord is my rock, my fortress and my deliverer; my God is my rock, in whom I take refuge, my shield and the horn of my salvation, my stronghold," (Psalm 18:2). And just like the parable Jesus would tell years later, Joseph, a wise and righteous man, had built his spiritual house upon God. When the rain came down, the streams rose, and the winds blew and beat against him, Joseph did not crumble because he had built his life on The Rock. Joseph wisely planned to obey what he knew of God's word, even though his heart was wrecked.

His life was characterized by a "long obedience in the same direction,"[9] and his obedience was pointed toward

God, regardless of the circumstances swirling about him.

Joseph sought to obey God, first by obeying the law, and then by accepting the relief of God's gracious message to him. *No wrong has been committed. There is no need for divorce. Your glad obedience is to marry her as planned.*

What a sweet grace for Joseph.

While some might ridicule us for obeying God's "irrelevant" commands, others might roll their eyes when we gratefully accept his grace. The only thing that can stabilize one's heart in such a fickle environment is to build our lives on the strong foundation of our unchanging God. And this is the guarantee: his unchanging grace will change us.

Receiving God's grace could be considered holy humiliation. We often hear that hard work is the only way to earn anything, and receiving an undeserved gift is disdained. We kick around slang words like *handout* and sling insults like *freeloader* and *leech*.

But to be a follower of Jesus is to suffer the humiliation of grace. His righteousness applied to my deficient account is an ongoing *handout*. As an heir of God and co-heir with Christ, I'm guaranteed to share his suffering and his glorious riches (See Romans 8:17). He delights to lavish gifts on spiritual freeloaders (See Ephesians 1:7-8). A leech sucks resources from a host. Although we cannot survive without being firmly attached to God, drawing our very breath and sustenance from him, his power to save and keep us will never—can never—be depleted.

Our responsibility is to follow him—to accept his light and easy burden and learn from him (See Matthew 11:29-30). When we do, obedience becomes a delight and an adventure no mere human could have dreamed.

❧

Oh, Lord,

Many times we feel unequipped and blindsided by your extraordinary plans. You don't require understanding, you require obedience. And it's a funny thing, in obedience you give peace, which is better than understanding circumstantial details.

Give us a heart like Joseph, who determined to obey you, first by following your law, then by accepting your grace.

Taking Mary Home

When Joseph woke up, he did what the angel of
the Lord had commanded him...

—Matthew 1:24

Joseph knocked on the door of Mary's father's house. The
sudden thumping roused their sleeping goat who had
been snuggled against the cool, stone wall. He scrambled
to his feet and scampered to the back of the house while
Joseph waited for someone to answer. He chewed his lip
and silently rehearsed the angel's words, *Do not be afraid.*
Was his churning stomach a result of fear or courage?
Neither, he decided. *This is obedience.*

Since they were pledged to be married, Mary was legally under his authority whether she lived in his house or
not. And though he knew his timing would be a surprise,
he would obey God and take Mary home as his wife.

Inside, someone struggled with the latch until and the

door scraped against the threshold. Mary's father stuck his bearded face through the opening then smiled and let him in. "Good morning, Joseph," he said. "This is unexpected."

Breakfast crumbs tumbled from his beard to his tunic with every syllable.

"Yes, I know." He hesitated for a moment, waiting to see if Mary was there. He smelled boiled eggs. Dried herbs hung over the stove seasoning the air. On the table, the remaining heel of a barley loaf begged for a bit of oil, and shadowed movements of busy women passed over it. "I've come to take Mary home as my wife. Our betrothal time is nearly over, and our room is finished. I am ready."

Mary's father chuckled. On hearing her name, Mary and her mother skittered in from the kitchen. Her mother was pale, and stammering, "but it's... we were... isn't it ..." Her expression pleaded with her husband to finish her sentences with words that would slow the jarring change of plans. But he didn't.

"Well, I suppose it's your privilege and right." Mary's father eyed him cautiously. "When do you intend for her to come?"

"Before the Sabbath."

Mary's mother whispered, "Before the Sabbath." Then she rushed back to the kitchen rearranging pots and glassware with a riotous clatter, setting her finest pieces on the table.

Mary's father opened his mouth to call his daughter

but stopped when he turned and saw her already listening.

"I'll be ready, Father," she said.

Her eyes were glassy with grateful tears, and she smiled at Joseph. With skin smooth as a polished stone and sun-kissed, Joseph resisted the impulse to touch her face. She was radiant, and she was his.

There was much they needed to tell each other. Joseph was eager to describe the angel, and now that he believed her, to hear about the angel who had visited her. No one else would believe him. Only Mary.

He had questions for her as well. Why was she gone so long at Elizabeth's? When would the baby come? What had she told her parents? Had she told them at all? Who else knew? Should they announce this wonder, or wait for folks to notice and then try to explain? Did she know his name?

These things warranted more discussion than a few moments in a doorway would allow, and bringing her to his home was the only acceptable way to do it. Besides, he'd been instructed by a messenger from God himself, and he was glad to obey.

For Joseph and Mary, and their families, the expected order of events had been shuffled. God had rearranged the plot points that would propel them toward the main event. The next step was clear, but the timing was surprising.

God had been so gracious to chase away uncertainty by sending angels so there would be no mistaking his will. Perhaps the best confirmation that Mary had not made it all up was the fluttering and stretching in her tummy. And sooner rather than later, Joseph would press his hand against a divine little elbow, straining against the fleshy confines of humanity. Together, they would marvel at the miracle from every angle.

Joseph surely knew the Psalm, "Your word is a lamp for my feet, a light on my path," (Psalm 119:105). When he finally brought Mary home, it was as if God's grace had shone a lamp on the next step of his journey. *This far for now, Joseph, take her home. Care for her and the baby.*

In our bright world, particularly at this time of year, blinding and blinking lights are never far away. When we think of God's word being a light to our path, we hope for sunlight, headlights, and spotlights. We want piercing brightness that shines far into the distance so we can see everything ahead.

So we know the dangers.

So we can see where the road turns and where it ends.

But God doesn't promise floodlights blazing into the uncertain future. If we could see all the obstacles at once, we'd be tempted to wriggle free of our Father's tender grasp and run ahead or run away.

If Joseph had known his commitment to raise Jesus with Mary would mean they'd obtain refugee status in Egypt, the quiet divorce he had considered might have seemed like a plausible escape. If Mary could have seen her son's future all the way to the cross, she'd have been plagued by three decades of terror.

To make it easier for us to keep our trembling hand in God's, he's given his word as a lamp, a small light illuminating the next steps. Often the next step is "wait." Sometimes it is "wait quietly." The next small step might be to get some rest or proper nourishment.

We do well to stay close to him by reading his word, observing what he reveals about himself, and listening for his caution and comfort. He can direct us because he sees the whole way to the end, even though we can't.

He's told us where he's going. He's bringing us along, and he knows how to get there, because actually, he *is* "the way the truth and the light," (John 14:6).

❧

Dear Lord,

Thank you for Joseph's example of courageous and immediate obedience. Give us the courage to follow your word without delay in the big and small things, whether we can see the way or not.

Day 19

A Higher Way

...and took Mary home as his wife. But he did not consummate their marriage until she gave birth to a son. And he gave him the name Jesus.

—Matthew 1:24

Still technically in their betrothal period, and yet married, Mary had moved her few belongings to Joseph's well-built house.

There wasn't much to bring. Just a small wooden chest whose latches rattled with every step. It held a few treasures from her mother: a linen tablecloth, permanently creased at the folds, two clay bowls and platters, a water pitcher, and a glass oil jar whose skinny neck was stuffed with a stopper. There was a goat-skin pouch for carrying water to the field or for traveling, and at the bottom of the chest, her wedding clothes cushioned all the breakables from their jostling trip across town.

Mary had arranged her dishes on the stone mantle above the stove. She tried to drape the linen cloth over the table Joseph had made. There were dents on its surface where the hammer had apparently missed its target. But when the creased cloth refused to lie flat, she decided the dented markings made it uniquely hers, and she hated to cover the lovely cedar woodgrain. She refolded the linen and put it back. Finally, she placed the pitcher and oil jar in the middle of the table and admired her quick work.

The rest she left in the chest. She scooted it to the corner and sat down on it while Joseph dusted the tabletop with his hand and tried, in vain, to buff out the dents with his sleeve. He sat on the floor beside her, leaned his head against the wall, and closed his eyes.

"Tell me about that angel." Joseph said. It was a tenuous request. He believed her, but it seemed almost too private a question.

Mary reviewed every unforgettable detail. "It scared me," she began. She told him about the angel's greeting, which made no sense to her at the time. She told him about Elizabeth and why she'd left in such a hurry. Then she told him the name. "We are to name him Jesus."

Joseph nodded but said nothing.

"Do you believe me, Joseph?"

He opened his eyes and looked at her. "I didn't at first... but I also saw an angel."

Mary studied him.

Joseph recounted how the angel had chased away his doubt and pointed him straight toward marriage on that tortuous yet wonderful night.

"Mary," he reached up to hold her hand, "we are the only ones in the world who know the Messiah's name."

"No one would believe it," she giggled and then sobered. It wasn't the only thing they wouldn't believe.

Nazareth would be counting the months and scratching their heads. Horrified accusations from family, friends, and neighbors were days away. As she worried and wondered, the prophet Isaiah's words came to mind:

> "For my thoughts are not your thoughts,
>
> neither are your ways my ways,"
>
> declares the LORD.
>
> "As the heavens are higher than the earth,
>
> so are my ways higher than your ways
>
> and my thoughts than your thoughts."
>
> (Isaiah 55:8-9)

Precious little was turning out as she once pictured. But God had graced her with a child. His child. Now he graced her with a confidant—Joseph. And she praised God because his ways were higher.

❧

In the beginning, before there was a nation called Israel, before distinctions between Jew and Gentile were delineated, before any Hebrew had uttered the word "Messiah," God had called him the Offspring and the Seed. God himself planted this hope that would put fallen humanity on alert for the Son he would send.

The Psalmists called him the Cornerstone, Deliverer and King. God's people would mistake these eternal characterizations as earthly ones. As such, they would fawn over temple rulers, military men, and palace royalty and would not even recognize their Servant King.

The prophet Isaiah called him the "Wonderful Counselor, Mighty God, Everlasting Father, Prince of Peace" (Isaiah 9:6). He was, and is, and will fulfill all those roles.

These titles, plus a host of others throughout the Old Testament, were arrows pointing the way to him, giving clues about where God's people would find the rescuer God had promised. They were indicators of what he would be like and the feats he would accomplish.

When he arrived, though, their long-awaited Messiah was called by other names.

His enemies slung racial insults[10] and accused him of being controlled by a demon from hell.[11] They drug his mother's character through the mud, insisting no one knew who had fathered him.[12] "We know this man is a sinner,"[13] they declared after he had given sight to a blind man. Even his brothers said he was out of his mind[14] and did not believe in him.[15]

In the gospels, he metaphorically called himself, the

Bread of Life, the Good Shepherd, and the Light of the World.

But Mary and Joseph called him Jesus, because that's what God told them to do.

Jesus means, "God saves." And because he died and rose to save us from our sins, you and I have the privilege of calling him Savior and Friend.

❧

Dear Lord,

Your ways are not our ways. Many times, we accuse you of being something you aren't instead of admitting our ignorance. We do not know you as well as we suppose. Help us turn from our own understanding and acknowledge your faithfulness to be exactly who you've claimed— our Saving God.

A Long Walk

All this took place to fulfill what the Lord had said through the prophet: "The virgin will conceive and give birth to a son, and they will call him Immanuel" (which means "God with us").

—Matthew 1:22-23

Her tummy had swollen.

The whole town had noticed.

And she and Joseph had been maligned.

Not yet twenty years old, and they were marked forever as adulterers. Though they were not.

Mary lumbered to the spring carrying the water jar on her disappearing hip.

It used to be a grand daily assignment. A walk with friends made the chore a happy one. But no one walked with her anymore. Her friends and their mothers walked far ahead or far behind as though she were contagious.

She had expected the reaction to some degree. God required holiness. As a nation they were called to be pure for him. Free from the stains of sin. In the days of Moses, they'd have stoned Joseph and her, regardless of their innocence.

Many of Nazareth's women were on their way back from the spring already. They corralled their children, especially their young daughters, and herded them to the side of the road opposite Mary. No greetings or polite smiles. No one offered a hand with the heavy jar. No one asked how many weeks she had left. And even though their reaction was to be expected, one day God would change their minds. For generations, people would say that she was blessed. But today, the loneliness, even among her family and neighbors, shocked her.

On her walk she fixed her mind on all the remarkable things God had done for Joseph and her. He'd chosen them to raise his Son, a deliverer for all of Israel, including their accusing neighbors. A rescuer was on his way. She smiled. *Someday they'll understand.*

Mary knelt to the spring and lowered her jar. It filled quickly. On her knees she pulled it from the water, steadied her unbalanced frame, then stood and hoisted it to her hip.

Sometimes she felt fragile, worn down by harsh words or silent shunning.

But at other times, she was worn out with so much

worship. When her unborn infant jabbed her in the ribs to wake her, she caught her breath. *How did God put you there?* She answered herself. "The Mighty One has done great things for me," and then she would list them until sleep returned.

On tiring days like today, when the night had been short and her praise had gone long, she borrowed melody and lyrics from King David. Gravel crunching under foot and water lapping at the jar composed a rhythm for her song. She returned from the spring alone singing:

"In you, LORD my God,

I put my trust.

I trust in you;

do not let me be put to shame,

nor let my enemies triumph over me.

No one who hopes in you

will ever be put to shame,

but shame will come on those

who are treacherous without cause.

Show me your ways, LORD,

teach me your paths.

Guide me in your truth and teach me,

for you are God my Savior,

and my hope is in you all day long."

(Psalm 25:2-5)

When we read of all the miraculous events and divine encounters, we may find ourselves a little envious of Mary and Joseph because of their remarkable conversations with angels. Like discontented children we cross our arms and huff, "...but God spoke so clearly to them..."

We whine and wish for the same celestial experiences, forgetting the angel spoke only once to Mary, and up to this point, only once to Joseph. Very little of the angelic messages made life "easier."

Everyone around them was inclined to operate under a normal, earthly understanding. Despite how Mary and Joseph may have explained, it was highly unlikely they were believed.

It is a stark reminder that God does not always choose the ho-hum path for the plans he has for us. We know he has "plans to prosper and not to harm. Plans to give us a hope and a future," (Jeremiah 29:11-13) as we are fond of quoting.

Did he have good plans for a prosperous future for Mary and Joseph? Who, on this side of redemptive history, would argue otherwise?

But there were undoubtedly seasons when the unexpected ways of God felt more like "harm" than "prospering." God does not evaluate circumstances through our myopic lens. His promise of certain hope and a guaranteed good future can be counted on. But God takes a wide view—the eternal view—of that future hope.

This sure hope is the birthright of believers. It is secured and kept in heaven for those of us who are shielded by God's power. Because we have such assurance, the apostle Peter writes, "In all this you greatly rejoice," but he quickly acknowledges that in the intervening time, "you may have had to suffer grief in all kinds of trials" (I Peter 1:6).

Most of life is walked out in that intervening time with sadness and hardships sprinkled throughout. But as God's children, we can be sure we're walking toward a bright future. Our "hope does not disappoint us because the love of God has been poured out within our hearts through the Holy Spirit who was given to us" (Romans 5:5, NASB). The Holy Spirit is God's invisible seal of ownership on you and me. He is a deposit and a proof of purchase, the guarantee of our future hope (Ephesians 1:14). And because he's with us and in us, we will never be truly hopeless, and we will never walk alone.

❧

Dear Lord,

A long obedience in the same direction is sometimes a lonely walk. But even so, you promise that those who wait for you will run and not grow weary, they will walk and not faint. Thank you for your strengthening presence.

A Devastating Decree

In those days Caesar Augustus issued a decree that a census should be taken of the entire Roman world. (This was the first census that took place while Quirinius was governor of Syria.) And everyone went to their own town to register.

—Luke 2:1-3

Joseph was quiet at the evening meal. His bread, soggy with oil, lay untouched on his plate. He rolled an olive between his fingers, then dropped it back into the bowl. He was anxious. Mary was too. She had been ravenous as she'd laid the table for supper, but after mopping up all the oil on her plate with one thick piece of barley loaf, she felt stuffed. She arched her back to gain some space to breathe, then she pushed away from table to inhale and sigh.

It was hard news at a hard time from a hard ruler. No one ever came to Nazareth on purpose. Sepphoris was a larger town and nearby, so travelers found necessities there. Most were glad to bypass Nazareth. But this morning, a group of horsemen dressed in Roman regalia galloped into Nazareth with news no one wanted to hear.

In the center of the village they halted and circled up. Sweaty horses stamped out their impatience and stirred the dust. Hearing an unapologetic shout to pay attention, village men emerged one by one from doorways and corrals. Boys gawked at the colorful plumes wobbling atop the soldier's helmets, and stared at each man's knife, which was sheathed and strapped to his muscular calf. Mothers shushed frightened children and hurried them indoors to hide.

One soldier stood in the stirrups, shook out a short length of scroll, and read the decree. His speech ran together with such bored familiarity that it was difficult to make out the individual words. Even so, there was no mistaking the message. Caesar Augustus, the Roman Emperor whose jurisdiction ran far and wide, had called for a census. A decree that meant traveling to one's ancestral town to be counted for taxes. Laughable and irrelevant as Nazareth was to the rest of the world, taxes could still be extracted from its residents, and Rome was glad to calculate the forthcoming revenue.

Another soldier dismounted, drove a stake into the

ground, and affixed the scroll as proof that Nazareth had been warned. Then they rushed out of the village, kicking up dust and dread as they rode away to declare the burden in the next village.

When the soldiers were out of sight, the men cursed the Romans, the women rushed from houses to see if they had heard correctly, and children peppered their parents with a hundred fascinated questions. *Do horses sneeze? What's a ceasar?*

Rome had had a history of executing far worse business than a census. But what would be taxed and how much? No one knew. Only one thing was certain, uncooperative citizens wouldn't have the privilege of worrying about it. Rome did not tolerate dissent.

"Have you ever been to Bethlehem?" Joseph asked dipping his bread into a plate of olive oil.

"Only as far as Jerusalem." Mary shrugged.

"I was there once when I was young." His smooth face was aged, not by time but by the lines in his brow and tensed jaw. "Many will be traveling. God will show us the way," he reassured.

Mary nodded. He was right of course. But it wasn't going to be easy.

Two days before the Sabbath, Mary ground barley and made bread. The next day she made more. While kneading, she laid plans. They would need food for at least a week. And oil if there was room. And water. At least two skins of water. The woolen blankets must be rolled and...

Her tummy tightened as she bent forward then back, pressing out flat loaves on the table. He's stretching, she thought. Or maybe he liked the rocking. Perhaps it was a soothing ride. She hoped he would feel the same on the back of a hobbling donkey.

⚘

All throughout Scripture we find evidence of the truth that "The king's heart is like channels of water in the hand of the Lord; He turns it wherever He wishes" (Proverbs 21:1, NASB). God has tapped a variety of historical rulers and leaders to participate in his great history.

The sad part is, so few of them realized it. God directed their actions according to his purposes—sometimes to judge, sometimes to bless. Nebuchadnezzar was allowed to bring judgement and catastrophe on God's people for their unbelief and disobedience (See Jeremiah 29:1-14). Cyrus was prompted to send the descendants of the chastised people back to their homeland for a fresh start (See Ezra 1:1-4).

Pilate was given the chore of condemning Jesus to death. And even as he tried to wash his hands of the responsibility, he was God's unknowing agent. Jesus himself told Pilate, "You would have no power over me if it were not given to you from above" (John 19:11).

And here, near his son's birthday, God tapped the shoulder of an unbelieving man, Caesar Augustus, who exposed his inflated ego by adding to his own name this title: "Son of the Divine."

God would use that devastating decree from an unbelieving king to provide a little reprieve to his obedient and heart-weary children. An escape to Bethlehem to grant relief and to fulfill prophecy. God wielded an empire, as John Piper points out, "to move two people seventy miles."[16]

And Mary and Joseph, in dutiful obedience to a lesser king, fulfilled the eternal plans of the Greatest King.

A quick glance into history reminds us we are governed by human leaders, but each of them are ultimately governed by and accountable to God. Whether they know it or not. Whether they believe it or not. And whether we witness the repercussions or not.

So, whether our human leaders have been established by God to judge or bless, we must remember, our first allegiance is to One Good King, the Everlasting Father, the Prince of Peace.

❧

Dear Lord,

Like Mary and Joseph, we have a dual
citizenship. Though we are glad servants in your
kingdom, we are still subject to lesser kings. Give
us wisdom to serve in such a way that even lesser
kings might glimpse your reign in us.

In the Shadow of a Fortress

So Joseph also went up from the town of Nazareth in Galilee to Judea, to Bethlehem the town of David, because he belonged to the house and line of David.

—Luke 2:4

With bruised heels and blistered toes, Joseph stumbled toward Bethlehem. The rolled bundle of provisions bounced against the donkey's rump and Mary's legs dangled over his flanks. Swollen flesh bulged between the straps of her sandals, like those of a large woman who spent her days on her feet. It did not agree with Mary's small frame.

Since they had hiked out of the valley south of

Jerusalem, Joseph had set his eyes on the high point of the horizon, an unnaturally shaped hill, it's top razed level and crowned with a fortress—Herod's palace. As they continued, its details came into focus.

Beyond the olive groves and terraced vineyards which lay between the palace and Joseph, a mere smudge came into view on the hillside landscape. Bethlehem. *Finally.* Nearly obscured in the shadows of Herod's regal monument to himself, it hardly looked fit to be the birthplace of the great King David.

Joseph imagined David as a boy among those hills tending sheep and composing music. It wasn't exactly a military training ground except for the wild animals he fought in defense of his father's flock. Joseph was struck again by the privilege, and the gravity, of raising royalty. *What did Jesse know about raising a king?* he asked himself. *Nothing.* God simply chose him. *And what do I know?* The answer was the same. Not a thing. But God had chosen Joseph too. And Mary. Their job was obedience. One weary step at a time.

He glanced back at Mary. Her eyes were squeezed shut, and her knuckles whitened around a tuft of mane. Other tired travelers converged on the road like tributaries trickling into the main channel as they all neared Bethlehem.

"Tonight, we'll sleep in a shelter," he encouraged. "We'll find the inn, first thing."

Mary did not respond, but the old man limping along

the trail in front of them did.

"Ha," he laughed, revealing the fact he'd overheard. Without looking back he added, "You'll be fortunate to find a cave."

Joseph was startled by the fellow's remark. As he surveyed the tiny village ahead, he forgot his ineptitude for raising a king and set his mind on simply providing for his wife. Scanning the hillside for an outcropping of rock to serve as cover just in case, Joseph repeated the confident lyrics of his ancestor, David. "For in the day of trouble he will keep me safe in his dwelling; he will hide me in the shelter of his sacred tent and set me high upon a rock" (Psalm 27:5).

He reached for the skin pouch of water that he'd slung over his neck and shoulder. It was nearly gone, and he'd almost forgotten it. "Mary," he said, and she opened her eyes.

He held it out to offer a drink, but she shook her head and closed her eyes again. "I can't."

It was at least a three-day journey from Nazareth to Bethlehem. As the crow flies, it was seventy miles. But Mary and Joseph weren't traveling as crows, and their journey through the hills and valleys of Judea made it even longer.

Bethlehem was, in the words of St. Luke, their "own city" because they were from the house and family of David. It was the town from which God had plucked a ruddy teenage shepherd boy and designated him as the future king.

From King David's family, and through his descendants, over years and generations, Joseph and Mary were eventually born. Then, at just the right time, by God's divine orchestration of human history, Joseph and Mary made their way back "home."

How ordinary Bethlehem was, but God's work makes ordinary people and out-of-the-way places memorable. A town known for its production of barley, *Bethlehem* meant "House of Bread." And unbeknownst to its livestock herders and Roman census officials, it was about to become the birthplace of the Bread of Life. Memorable indeed.

This is good news for regular people like you and me. God does not ask us to work hard in order to make a name for ourselves. He has not even asked us to be successful.

God asks ordinary people to be faithful to him—to be willing and fully committed to listen to him and obey. We stay the course, with our eyes locked on the destination he has chosen, even if it looks like a smudge on the landscape or a small and unremarkable place.

It is God's work that transforms ordinary people and

places into memorable names that point back to him.

He gets the glory, and we get the joy of remembering and reporting all he has done.

❧

Dear Lord,

You grant what you require. You prepare for your plan. Our privilege is to trust and receive. Our challenge is to accept your accommodations without complaint.

Though you may protect us in the cleft of a rock rather than a home, though you hide us with your hand rather than fortress walls, your unconventional ways allow us to glimpse your glory and sense your presence. And though we may ignorantly complain at first, we wouldn't want it any other way.

Day 23

A Bethlehem Emergency

He went there to register with Mary, who
was pledged to be married to him and was
expecting a child.

—Luke 2:5

Bethlehem churned with activity. The town was unequipped for sojourning masses. Small groups huddled
around small fires at the end of streets and between buildings. Bed rolls had been laid out haphazardly along the
edge of the street, and Joseph's heart sank. Travelers were
exhausted. Villagers were irritated. And with the Romans
milling through the chaos, everyone was on edge.

Joseph waited in line to register his name and family. In front of them two children whined and thread-
ed themselves between their parents who, though they
whispered, were clearly arguing. He debated whether he
would prefer taxation for the rest of his life, or a life cut

short by military service. Caesar wanted one or the other, soldiers or silver. Perhaps he was counting both. Why else would Caesar want to measure his dominion?

Between the buildings a dog barked suddenly, and the donkey's head jerked upward. Mary whimpered. He'd been so engrossed in his musings he hadn't noticed her pale complexion.

"Mary?" He laid his hand on hers. Still gripping the mane, her hand was cold and trembling.

"Joseph … I think the baby is coming."

Joseph felt the blood drain from his face.

"Are you sure?"

"No. But it hurts."

Joseph immediately stepped out of line and led the donkey away from the crowd. *It was too much for her. We should have stayed with Zechariah and Elizabeth to rest for a day. Or more.* Joseph looked up and down the street for a guest house.

With the sun setting, a group of strangers gathered in front of a large house clamoring for rooms. *That's it.* He walked beside the donkey with one hand on Mary and the other prodding the donkey forward. Her eyes were pressed tight, and under her shawl, beads of sweat glistened on her forehead.

Joseph was scared. There was no time for waiting.

Tradition would keep him from calling out to the patron of the guest house. But fright and urgency trumped tradition.

"Do you have a room?" he cried from the back when the owner appeared. Everyone stared. Mary's condition was urgent and obvious.

The man shook his head, and Mary began to cry.

Oh, God, deliver your servant.

❧

Mary and Joseph were favored. Graced. Righteous.

And yet they were caught up in an emergency.

All the unfavorable circumstances mocked their radical obedience. They were young, unexperienced, far from home, exposed to elements of the outdoors, and enduring an crisis right in front of strangers. Whether it was cold or dirty or both, it was likely not the "birth plan" they had in mind.

It's not much fun to ponder the emergencies God allows. We'd much rather adore him as the God who prevents catastrophe.

And he does. The near miss. The misdiagnosis. The perfect timing.

But he is also undeniably the God who allows them. He allows his children to wonder and cry.

Why?

Perhaps it is because the wondering turns our face towards his, and the crying brings us to his shoulder where he can remind us that he is our caring Father who is near-by, even in our emergencies.

⁂

Dear Lord,

You are not surprised by urgent needs. Emergencies do not catch you off guard. You have already been to the place you provide, vacating the stable, clearing out the manger, pointing the way to the entrance, covering our urgent cries with grace.

A Most Unlikely Midwife

While they were there, the time came for the baby to be born...

—Luke 2:6

The owner of the guest house pointed out the stable where the other travelers had tied their animals. Joseph threw open the rickety gate and halted the donkey. Mary draped her arms over his shoulders, and he helped her slide from the donkey's back to her feet. Supporting Mary, he had no way to tie the donkey. He left it and guided her further inside where she could lie down.

Though no one in the long line had wanted to step away and lose their place, a servant girl came running from the guest house into the stable, startling the donkey and causing the few sheep to start bleating. Their pitiful cry echoed off the stone walls of the stable, grating on Joseph's frayed nerves, and for a moment Joseph considered turning them loose.

The servant looked older than both of them, but not by much. "Is this the firstborn?" she asked.

Joseph's throat was dry. The donkey had followed them to the back, and, as Joseph's hands were shaking, he fumbled to tie up the reins. His youth and inexperience were exposed. He felt like a boy and not a man. "Yes," he replied.

She gave him a pitcher of water and bowl of salt. He spilled them both with his quaking. She draped a pile of long rags over his shoulder and said, "Sounds like she's almost ready. Send to the house if you need something," and she rushed back inside.

Send who? Joseph put the remaining salt and water down and knelt in the puddle where he'd spilled them.

With her body curved toward the baby she was bringing, Mary writhed in pain. She had told him about Elizabeth's delivery, and now every detail of that description was coming to life. *God, is this how you bring your Son into the world? In the dark, with bleating sheep, to a crying woman and a terrified man? This isn't the place for a King.*

His frantic questioning opened the floodgates of worry which could only be shut with a rehearsal of what he knew for sure. "The eyes of the Lord are on the righteous," he said it aloud to reassure them both, "and his ears are attentive to their cry" (Psalm 34:15).

Almost afraid to touch her for fear he'd make it worse, he lightly wiped her forehead with the rags. She held her breath and bore down again. Her lips were purple, almost gray, and Joseph begged her to inhale. "Breathe," he whispered, and she gasped and sobbed.

❧

It's hard to imagine that in God's sovereignty, with his foreknowledge, and according to the plan he designed before time began, he chose a dark, dirty, and dangerous setting.

And he did it on purpose. Clearing out the delivery room of busy guests, distracted workers, and bringing a quiet peace to bustling Bethlehem.

There in the shelter of what many believe was more a cave than a barn, God assembled the little family he'd chosen for his Son.

The frightened stepfather wondering and praying.

The highly favored mother sweating and crying, holding her breath and gasping.

And Himself, The Great I AM, silent and present.

The invisible God, watching and working as the baby who was "the image of the invisible God" was pushed into history, wearing the confines of human flesh. He who invisibly stood by orchestrated every detail behind the scenes.

In a tiny country, a tiny town, a tiny cave to a tiny girl, all the fullness of Deity was compacted into a tiny baby. The bigness of God in the smallness of human flesh to be our Prince of Peace.

Peace amid turbulent, unexpected circumstances can only be explained as God's peace. God's Peace, as the Apostle Paul wrote, "surpasses understanding" (See Philippians 4:7). Peace that comes from knowing God's word and trusting his undeniable presence is better than understanding the *hows* and *whys* of the crisis in the moment.

The assurance of his presence also provides a sense of calm that can't be explained.

If we desire to be faithful, chosen, and used for God's glorious plan, we can expect a sometimes-harrowing ride. Though God uses ordinary people, his plans are rarely predictable.

But he gives peace to comfort and calm us in unexplainable ways even in the midst of his extraordinary plan.

❧

Dear Lord,

You deliver your servants. Sometimes by the help of others, sometimes by your presence alone, sometimes by giving peace that is beyond understanding. We are grateful we belong to you.

Day 25

The Savior is Born

...and she gave birth to her firstborn, a son. She wrapped him in cloths and placed him in a manger, because there was no guest room available for them.

—Luke 2:7

Mary shivered violently. Joseph unrolled their two woolen blankets and wrapped them around her. She lay on her side, her newborn cradled in the crook of her arm. Joseph was overheated with fear. He lay down beside her and, drawing close, pressed his warmth against the wool. Still, she shook. Was it from the cold or the trauma? Joseph didn't know.

"Are you cold or frightened?" he asked.

"Both. But I'm warming up." He raised his head to peek over her shoulder to see the baby Son of God.

Jesus.

He had come into the world silently at first, bloody and blue and Joseph had almost screamed. Lambs were sometimes lethargic after birth, but never blue, and it was all he had to compare it with. But within moments, the baby had given a squalling protest to the cold air, and Joseph breathed relief. Mary swaddled him in cloths to dry and warm him just as Elizabeth's midwife had done.

Jesus was quiet and warm now. His shiny black hair stuck flat to his head, and he was still, except for that little indention in the middle of his head where Joseph could see the beating of a divine pulse.

Mary was weak and Joseph was mystified. *Is this how babies arrive? Does life cost so much blood?*

"Joseph, I need to sleep."

Mary pushed herself up on an elbow and carefully laid the swaddled baby in the empty feeding trough. Joseph cringed and tucked the last clean rag under the tiny bundle.

Mary collapsed into sleep, and Joseph sat up as though he was the night watchman. He was exhausted but far from sleeping.

Mary and Jesus lay motionless. In the dim light of the flickering oil lamp Joseph stared at one then the other.

"King Jesus," Joseph whispered, as if to try it on.

Not in Jerusalem, but in Bethlehem.

Not a palace, but a stable.

Not a throne, but a feeding trough.

Not an entourage, but a teenage couple.

No one heralding his arrival except a lonely descendant of David whispering his divine title.

King Jesus.

⁂

What a precious glimpse God has preserved for us through his word. More than likely it was Mary's own account told three decades later to the apostle Peter and passed on from him to the writer, Luke.

In a few short verses God has allowed us to peer through a crack in the wall to see just a few of the details of that night.

Imagine Joseph hovering over Jesus' little body— quick and quiet breathing pumping his newborn chest up and down.

Imagine Joseph worshiping in adoring Hebrew whispers, "Yeshua."

On this first Christmas, just moments after Jesus was born, it probably appeared to Joseph that the long-expected Messiah had arrived at an inappropriate place with no fanfare or announcement at all.

But just as God has somewhat hidden from us those first moments with the Infant King, he had hidden from Joseph many future events.

Joseph did not yet know there was a choir of angels

stirring up a ruckus on a hillside in that region.

He did not yet know musky shepherds were hustling toward the awkward sight of a baby in a feeding trough. He did not yet know the blessing of Anna or Simeon or of the looming "sword" that would pierce Mary's soul. He did not yet know the wise men's gifts would also agitate the paranoia of an insane king. He did not yet know his little family would need to flee for their lives under a genocidal decree from that same ruler.

But he knew Jesus was God's Son, born to save his people from their sins.

And for Joseph, at this moment, that was all God chose to show him.

And it was enough.

In a sense, you and I are living in that same space—between the wonder of all God has done and all the trials and glory to come.

We know about the manger, the cross, and the empty tomb. The rest he promised is still somewhat hidden.

We do not know when we'll hear the diagnosis or a dreaded announcement. We do not yet know every detail about angels, or the particulars of Heaven, or the exact implications of an eternal Kingdom.

Though we cannot fathom the extent of future hardships or blessings, we know Jesus and he know us.

And that is everything we need for now.

❧

Dear Lord,

You have veiled that sacred night leaving us with so few details. The particulars of the moment that divides history, you have kept private. But its implications you have declared as Good News to all people.

The Israelites waited more than four hundred years for deliverance through two water-walls, and over four hundred years for your promised Deliverer—a baby. And we are waiting now, some two thousand years later, for your glorious appearing when every knee will bow and proclaim, "King Jesus!"

Even so, Lord Jesus, come.

Good News of Great Joy

And there were shepherds living out in the fields nearby, keeping watch over their flocks at night. An angel of the Lord appeared to them, and the glory of the Lord shone around them, and they were terrified. But the angel said to them, "Do not be afraid. I bring you good news that will cause great joy for all the people. Today in the town of David a Savior has been born to you; he is the Messiah, the Lord. This will be a sign to you: You will find a baby wrapped in cloths and lying in a manger."... But Mary treasured up all these things and pondered them in her heart.

—Luke 2:8-12,19

Mary woke to Jesus' soft cry. She sat up in halting movements, shifting her aching frame until she could reach him.

She slid her hand between the baby and the feeding trough. Holding him close, she did everything she had seen Elizabeth do, and nursed him back to sleep.

She couldn't help but wonder why God meant for his son to be born in the dank shelter of a cave, but she marveled at God's continual gifts:

That she, of all girls, was mother of the Savior; that God would bring her to Elizabeth and her celebrating friends to learn everything a new mother should know; that he would tell Joseph she was not an adulterer; that Joseph married her in thankful obedience.

And now, as she had dreaded giving birth under the scrutinizing eye of Nazareth, God had dispatched a Roman decree to give respite from the scorn. Though she lay near the cold wall of a stable cave, sapped of strength, her worship came through tears, the only gift she had to offer for all she'd received.

Joseph lay limp beside her, undisturbed by the baby, and not wakened by her first attempts to nourish God's Son. He was a good husband. And a tired one. She smiled and swallowed the lump in her throat.

Laying Jesus back in the feeding trough, she eased herself down again. She was just on the edge of sleep when she heard scuffling near the entrance. Her eyes shot open but there was nothing to see in the dark. She heard it again.

And voices too.

She shook Joseph's shoulder. "Joseph." He woke

with a start.

"Someone's out there."

Her heart thumped wildly. Bethlehem's influx of people seeking to follow the law inevitably brought those who weren't. She couldn't run. She wasn't sure she could stand. She scooted toward Jesus and pulled Joseph's arm toward her.

"Tell them we have nothing worth taking," she whispered. But Joseph sat silent, still trying to determine what or who or how many.

Then a torch flickered at the entrance. "Anybody in here?" A gravelly voice startled them all, including the sheep and they started bleating again.

A bearded skeleton of a man made his way in. He lifted the torch, and his eyes grew wide. From his toothless smile a wheezing laugh erupted. He hollered over his shoulder, "He's in here."

Frightened and confused, Joseph asked, "What do you want?"

"We just wanted to see if it was true. A baby king in a trough." He chuckled. "Just like he said."

"Who said?" Mary asked as several scroungy men crowded in. She felt uneasy and confused. And sore. She wanted to lie down.

"The angel."

He was so matter of fact, and considering the events of the past nine months, neither Mary nor Joseph questioned it.

"When... where... I mean, what did he say?" Joseph asked.

The first men who had entered were scooting aside as several more scuttled in to have a look. *How many are there?* Mary wondered. *How did they find us? How do they know?*

"Well, we was tendin' all our flock outside town. When all-a-sudden the whole sky just lit up like a fire. There was a shinin' man... well, not a man... an angel, I think. I been workin' sheep my whole life, and I never seen any angel till tonight." He nodded toward his fellow shepherds. "Some of 'em started runnin' so he come and hollered, 'Don't be afraid!' Well, it was too late."

Mary leaned forward. Captivated. An angel had announced where and when and who and described their embarrassing situation: her baby—God's Son—lying in a feeding trough, of all places. *Dear God, is this where you meant us to be?*

"Then a whole herd of 'em showed up praisin' God." He exhaled a wheezing laugh again and paused. "Then... well, the night sky just kinda... opened up and they went back up where they come from."

The rest of the shepherds nodded in solemn agreement.

"So, we knowed this was the Christ, and we come as fast as we could."

Mary sat stunned.

"You believe us, miss?" one of them asked.

"Oh, yes." Mary answered quietly.

But would anyone else?

Taking one more look at her baby and surveying the ill-fitting room, the shepherds began leaving the cave, one by one. Excited chatter echoed in the night, and Mary hoped the Romans were asleep.

"Hey!" She heard one shepherd yell, "Know what we seen tonight?"

And she knew the news was out.

⅋

Dear Lord,

How fitting that you would send local shepherds to identify the Lamb of God in a stable where lambs were kept. How familiar the surroundings and yet how unexpected.

⅋

No one caught their names. In human estimation they were nameless livestock workers doing the mundane and dirty work of leading their flock to tufts of grass and nearby streams and caring for sheep every day and night in all kinds of weather.

But these men, with dirt and oil under their nails, smelling as much like sheep as their herd, were the ordinary people God chose to spread the word concerning what had been told them about this child. The Lamb of God in a feed box was the Savior they'd been awaiting.

It was good news for all people. They couldn't keep quiet about it and everyone who heard it was amazed.

For many years, I could identify with the ordinary shepherds, but I did not have their delight. My spreading the word concerning Jesus, or "sharing the gospel" or "witnessing" as it's called, felt more like an embarrassing chore than a delightful privilege.

To me, the gospel was only "kind of good news." Maybe more like "okay news." I'd grown up in church and come through decades of Sunday school, Wednesday night school, and Vacation Bible school. I even earned a degree in Biblical Studies. And somehow, with all the head knowledge, the gospel was just "okay news" I felt obligated to share, occasionally.

By age five, I knew God was holy, I was a sinner and that Jesus came to bridge the gap between God and me. His cross made a way for me to go to Heaven someday.

In my earliest memories of Sunday school, I sat on a thin carpet square in an echoing church classroom. The industrial carpet was brilliant turquoise and smelled of antique basement. Other children wriggled in close as my mom told the Bible story of a little boy who gave his five barley loaves and two fish to Jesus. With them, Jesus fed a meadow full of people. She distributed color-ful postcards with a vivid image of the scene that trans-ported me to that hillside.

With child-like faith, I believed.

But I felt like I was an annoying bother who required too much forgiveness. Like a child knocking on the door of an irritated neighbor asking, again to be allowed in his fenced backyard to retrieve a ball, I hung my head and covered my face. It had to be done, but shame on me for letting it happen.

Because God had been so merciful to save and prom-ise me Heaven someday, I spent decades striving to earn his favor and trying not to disappoint him. Trying not to deplete his forgiveness.

Trouble was, I liked my sin, and I was such a disap-pointment to myself, I decided I needed to shore things up with God and build in a little cushion between us. So, I opened an imaginary checking account with him. I would make deposits I thought he'd approve of. I'd read my Bible, memorize verses, attend church, confess sin, encourage a friend, obey my parents (sometimes), and es-tablish a pretty hefty balance.

When I arbitrarily decided I'd made enough deposits, I granted myself permission to make a withdrawal—to ask God for something. I'd pray for things I wanted—good grades from average study habits, safety while bar-reling down gravel roads to my violin lesson, cute boys to pay attention. If my requests weren't granted, I figured I'd overdrawn my account somehow. Maybe there wasn't enough to cover the withdrawal in the first place.

Mine was a transactional faith, completely dependent upon the quality of my performance. Determining factors that granted approval were arbitrary, unpredictable, and far from "good news" that I was supposed to be sharing. By this time, I was an apathetic wife, a grouchy mother, and a shell of a Christian.

Until one day.

I was tired. Tired of meeting needs and feeling needy. Tired of being a grump and dealing with grumpy kids. Tired of trying so hard to be a faithful Christian example and failing so often. Tired of praying for things to get better while circumstances remained unchanged.

After laying my kids down for a nap, I tiptoed over squeaky floorboards toward my living room and accidentally kicked a mound of unmatched socks. Books I meant to read were piled on my side table. My Bible lay opened on the ottoman, with red pen scribbled across the ninety-first Psalm and a three-year-old's signature scrawled over the footnotes.

Collapsing in my armchair, I began to cry. Not loudly, of course. I didn't want to wake the nappers, which made the shoulder-shaking, headache-inducing cry that much more miserable. Overwhelming physical and spiritual fatigue required release, but it had to be silent if I wanted to have my cry all alone. And I did.

I'd been reading to my kids from our Children's Bible at nights. The disconnect between the heroes of the faith we read about and the disaster of my own faith made me feel like a slimy hypocrite.

Over the years, my childlike faith had been eclipsed by a drive to earn favor and build up that balance. I thought if I "did hard things" and if I "let go and let God" and performed everything "right" then everything would turn out like I wanted it to. Inspiration plucked from coffee mugs and bumper stickers had stacked up in my soul alongside misapplied scriptures like so many unmatched socks.

If I was striving to please God in the regular work of mothering, then why was it so hard? And why was everything turning out so badly?

Friends of mine were doing really hard things—homeschooling, parenting large families or medically fragile children, even building orphanages in Haiti.

I was barely making it to church. It wouldn't be a stretch to say that the free childcare provided by the nursery might have been my main reason for attending church during that season. "Everyone else" was performing remarkable acts of faith and ministry, and I could barely boil macaroni.

I began to suspect that something was wrong with my faith. I was disappointed with myself, and certain God was disappointed in me too. The Bible heroes my kids and I read about were giant-slayers, ark-builders, and sea-crossers.

Followers of Jesus were supposed to be great performers like that.

Weren't they?

Thumbing through our Jesus Storybook Bible, I read this shocking statement by Sally-Lloyd Jones, "the people God uses don't have to know a lot of things or have a lot of things—they just have to need him a lot."

Now there was a qualification I could meet. But I didn't completely trust the "children's Bible." Over the next few months I read through the gospels in my grownup Bible, and I discovered, to my astonishment, the same clarifying truth.

Throughout the gospels Jesus regularly commented about people's faith. But they weren't the people you'd expect. They were some of the most unlikely "heroes" in the Bible. We don't know their names. We only know them by their afflictions—the hemorrhaging woman, the Samaritan leper, the paralytic. What did Jesus notice about them when they crossed his path? Their disease? Their interruption?

Maybe.

But the thing he remarked about—even marveled at— was their faith. The fact was indisputable: they were people who knew they needed Jesus a lot. They brought him their desperate needs, and he commended their faith.

For many of us, somewhere between the carpet squares of Sunday school and the living room chair, the good news has become unrecognizable. Growing up means doing things yourself, becoming independent, and achieving more. But faith in Jesus is not a matter of great, independent achievements.

The good news of Jesus' incarnation, life, death, and resurrection is more than a spiritual bank account.

There is an account, so to speak, but it was opened long before I decided the terms of use. And for believers in Jesus, there is a single recorded transaction.

When Jesus died on the cross, the ledger filled with my sin—pride, worry, earning, and love for secret sins, to name a few—was effectively deleted. "He canceled the record of the charges against us and took it away by nailing it to the cross" (Colossians 2:14, NLT). He suffered the punishment I had earned.

But that was only the first part of the transaction.

He didn't leave the ledger empty. Although the account bears my name, the ledger bears the record of someone else. It is filled with the righteousness of Christ and credited to me as though it were mine. And what is required of me? Believe what he says. "This righteousness is given through faith in Jesus Christ to all who believe" (Romans 3:22). His perfect life, his performance, permanently secured God's favor toward me.

This was the "good news" that I had somehow missed for so many years. "For God made Christ, who never sinned, to be the offering for our sin, so that we could be made right with God through Christ" (2 Corinthians

5:21, NLT).

My striving to earn God's favor, to keep my account full, was needless. Jesus had earned God's favor for me. Continually berating myself for confessed sin was completely unnecessary. Jesus had suffered the punishment for it, served the sentence for me, and declared, "It is finished."

In God's sight my record is stamped, "Approved!" And if you believe his work was enough, yours is too.

God's grace—his unearned favor—is an overwhelming relief. This is the one true gospel and it's the point where Christian life begins. It is exceedingly good news of great joy for all people. And it's a delight to join the shepherds in returning to our ordinary lives, glorifying and praising God for everything he has done, which is exactly what he promised to do.

He has saved his people.

Glory to God in the highest.

Acknowledgements

This little book has had a long gestation.

In 2012, I was writing Christmas letters and exchanging hilarious email correspondence with my dear college friends, Pearl and Manel (Our collective first initials forming the unforgettable acronym P.M.S.), when I discovered I enjoyed writing. Since I had spent most of my high school and college days dreading and avoiding papers and essays, this came as a shock.

I also discovered writing is a skill requiring practice, and there is no such thing as a good writer—only bad writers who didn't quit. So, to practice and continue, I accepted an annual online challenge to write every day for thirty-one days in a row. On day eight, I stalled.

In 2013, I tried again, this time with a focus and a plan. By draping the fabric of imagination over the framework of the biblical Christmas story, I retold the familiar story one day at a time on my blog. The first thirteen days were a delight, but I slogged through the remaining days, eventually quitting on day twenty-four, because it was Christmas Eve, and I doubted anyone was reading anyway.

In January, I bumped into a man from church who "confessed" that he had read the entire series on Christmas Eve. He loved it and said, "How did you do that?" I was shocked, and I didn't know exactly what he meant, but I supposed I should polish it and post it again the next Christmas.

Each year it evolved. Nonfiction reflections were added. It received a digital book cover, and the next year, an upgraded cover. Every year I offered it as a gift to anyone who wanted to download the digital file. And every year I'd receive emails asking if it was in print.

Now it is, and I have many people to thank.

To early readers who wrote me to say they were encouraged or changed, who shared their love for the e-book with friends and family, thank you!

To those who've asked, and waited patiently, for a book with paper pages and a spine, thank you. E-books are wonderfully economic to produce and distribute, but I will always prefer a printed book, which never needs to be charged.

To all who have read, prayed, printed the e-book on your own printer, your encouragement has fueled my love for writing and Bible study.

To Yolanda Smith, voracious reader, talented writer, and gracious editor, thank you for your time and generosity. You inspire and amaze, and your friendship is a gift.

To Taryn Nergaard, your design wizardry leaves me slack-jawed. Thank you.

To Kurt, my husband and "proud sponsor" of all my blogging and book writing ventures, you're a keeper. I'm gratefully yours.

To my Savior, I don't know why you'd allow me the luxury of trying to imagine unrecorded details of your incarnation, but I thank you. It was a pleasure and a delight. I'm so looking forward to hearing how it really happened... someday.

Notes

Return to Wonder

1. Barbara Robinson, The Best Christmas Pageant Ever (New York, NY: Avon, 1972), pg. 55.

Righteous and Childless

2. Alfred Edersheim, The Life and Times of Jesus the Messiah (Grand Rapids, MI: AP & A,) pg. 105.

Faithful to the Holy

3. Psalm 118:24
4. Psalm 51:2, NLT
5. Psalm 24:7-8
6. Psalm 139:23-24

An Inconceivable Conception

7. Psalm 132:12

An Unbelievable Predicament

8. See Luke 1:30-38

Joseph Gets the Message

9. Eugene Peterson likens Christian discipleship to "a long obedience in the same direction," and has written a book titled, A Long Obedience in the Same Direction: Discipleship in an Instant Society. (Downers Grove, IL: IVP Books, 2000, second edition), p. 17. It is a description he has quoted from Friedrich Nietzsche in Beyond Good and Evil.

A Higher Way

10. See John 8:48
11. See John 8:52
12. See John 8:41
13. John 9:24
14. See Mark 3:21
15. See John 7:5

A Devastating Decree

16. Jon Piper, "All God's Little People," accessed 8/28/19 https://www.desiringgod.org/articles/for-gods-little-people

About the Author

Shauna Letellier weaves strands of history, theology, and fictional detail into a fresh retelling of familiar Bible stories on her blog and in her books. With her husband Kurt, she has the wild and hilarious privilege of raising three boys along the banks of the Missouri River where they fish, swim, and rush off to ball games.

Download a free devotional at shaunaletellier.com/freedevo or connect with Shauna online at Facebook or Instagram.

Also by Shauna Letellier

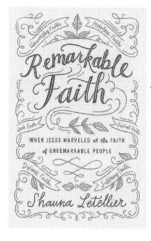

Remarkable Faith: When Jesus Marveled at the Faith of Unremarkable People

Remarkable Hope: When Jesus Revived Hope in Disappointed People

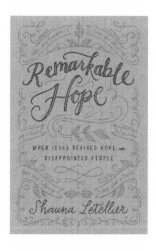

Download her free devotional at
shaunaletellier.com/freedevo

Available wherever books & ebooks are sold.

10156917R00116

Manufactured by
Amazon.ca
Bolton, ON